YOUR CATHOLIC LANGUAGE

YOUR
CATHOLIC LANGUAGE

LATIN FROM THE MISSAL

BY

MARY PERKINS

SHEED & WARD
NEW YORK & LONDON
1940

NIHIL OBSTAT

ARTHUR J. SCANLAN, S.T.D.

Censor Librorum

IMPRIMATUR

✠ FRANCIS J. SPELLMAN, D.D.

Archbishop, N. Y.

New York, February 16, 1940

AMERICAN BOOK—STRATFORD PRESS, INC., NEW YORK

To

OUR LADY

TABLE OF CONTENTS

FOR WHOM THIS BOOK IS DESIGNED

Those who know no Latin.

Those who know some Latin, but not enough to feel at home with the Liturgy.

Those who are learning classical Latin, and would like to apply their knowledge in daily life.

Those who are teaching classical Latin to Catholics.

WHY LEARN LATIN?

The early Christians spoke to God in their own language.

Later, Latin came to be the language only of the educated.

Our democratic ideal is that everyone can and should be educated, that is, should be equipped with the tools to educate himself.

Every Catholic of the Roman Rite who shares this ideal owes himself a knowledge of Ecclesiastical Latin, because:

Every Catholic who is educated in the things of the world, can and should be even more cultured in the things of God.

Latin is the language of the Church, as we know Her.

We will feel more at home in the Church if we can use Her language without interpretations and translations.

The original is always superior to the translation, especially in such a close-knit, exact language as Latin.

Church Latin was evolved from the language of the people to meet the need for exact theological and devotional expression. Therefore, in learning and savoring the language of the Liturgy, we are learning theology, and increasing devotion.

Church Latin is not a "dead" language. The official business of the Western Church is transacted in Latin. The literature of the Church—Propers of Masses, Encyclicals of the Popes—is still growing. Latin is used as an international language by priests, seminarians, missionaries. (In China, Christians use it as an every-day language, since they do not understand each other's dialects.)

Therefore, a knowledge of Church Latin is one of the best tools for continuous self-education in the mind of the Church.

WHY NOT LEARN LATIN?

You know a great deal already, even if you have never studied Latin.

If you have ever studied it, even unwillingly, you will find you remember a great deal more than you would think.

It is one of the languages from which our own is derived. Most of its words have English derivatives. Therefore there is comparatively little vocabulary trouble.

It is the most consistent language of which we have any knowledge. The irregular verbs are not more numerous than the regular, and there are very few irregularities of any kind.

Most of the rules of grammar are rules of common sense, and there are comparatively few that must be learned.

All its sounds are contained in English speech, so you do not have to learn any new ones.

The worst part of any language study is, for most people, the English-into-whatever-it-is exercises. You will not find any of those here.

A small amount of effort leads to a disproportionately large reward.

You will not have wasted whatever time you spend on it, even if you do not go through the whole book. Whatever you have learned will stay with you, as you will use it every time you go to Mass.

HOW TO USE THIS BOOK

You can read it straight through, as if it were a novel, which may give you a general feeling of "How interesting!" but not much more.

You may want Latin to be merely an acquaintance, not a friend, in which case, read only the left-hand pages.

If you actually want to learn Latin, so that you could understand a new Collect, or an Encyclical, or a page of St. Augustine as easily in Latin as in English, you will have to read the whole book, and follow all the suggestions given.

The Latin of the Mass, with a literal interlinear translation, is given on the left-hand pages.

The purpose is to **understand** Latin, not to translate it, so do not try to rearrange it into an English order of words. Take it as it comes. Read the Latin (aloud, if possible). You probably know how to pronounce it already, but in case you do not, or would like to be sure you are right, see p. 160. Look at the translation and find out what each word means. Look at the English derivatives given below and see how many of the Latin words are already familiar to you.

Then read the Latin over again until the meaning of each sentence comes to you directly from the Latin, without any English intermediary. It may seem difficult at first, but in time the sense of any Latin sentence will come to you as directly as does that of "Dominus vobiscum", if you use and persevere in this direct Latin-to-you approach.

But two kinds of knowledge are needed in order to be at home in a language: the actual meaning of words used—Vocabulary, and the method of putting words together—Syntax, or ordering. As

3

most of the actual vocabulary of ecclesiastical Latin is familiar to us, the only thing necessary is to make conscious use of this familiarity. In giving English derivatives from Latin words, the purpose is to show both the samenesses and the differences in the meaning of the Latin word, and the present meaning of its derivatives.

On the right-hand pages, you will find the second kind of information. You will be working with real Latin, not with sentences made up for the purpose, so that you will not be able to understand at once why every word in any sentence is as it is. The advantage of such a method is that you will really want the explanation when it is given, and therefore you will be more apt to remember it.

All tables of declensions and conjugations are at the back of the book, to be referred to only when you are convinced of their necessity.

It is cheering to remember that Language existed before Grammarians. Latin had been spoken and written for centuries before anyone began to classify its words and to tell people how they ought to use them. Rules of grammar and syntax are like the Common Law: they merely tell you in legal form what has been going on for a long while.

The advantage of learning this common law of a foreign language is that it enables you to grasp the reasons for a great many things at the same time. It would be possible to explain it without using any technically grammatical terms, but it would take much more space and be less satisfactory. There is nothing frightening about a technical term, as such. It is either the best, or the generally accepted tool for its job, and once you know what it means, you can use the tool as well as anyone. Grammatical terminology is a fascinating mixture of functionalism and metaphor, and once you have really grasped it, you can use it for any language, including your own.

You will find that one subject is explained at a time, with all that you need to know about that subject. At first you will probably feel as if you were trying to tidy up somebody else's top bureau drawer, because there will be so many things in the Latin text, about which you do not as yet know anything, surrounding the one thing you are trying to learn. This situation will improve itself in time, and you will find at the end of the book that everything is sorted out into neat divisions. When this begins to come true, go back and read the first part over again. You will probably find many things in it that you did not see the entire reason for, or use of, which will all come clear then.

If you have never studied any Latin, it will, of course, take more time for you to become familiar with case-endings and such. But if you do a very small amount of memory work, and remember to apply it to the Latin text as indicated, you will find that all these case-endings and verb forms are not half so formidable as they may seem to be. The first part will be the worst, especially if you have never thought much about Why Grammar, but it should all improve suddenly somewhere near the middle of the book.

You will find a summary at the end of each section of the things with which you should be familiar at that point. Do not worry if you are not familiar with everything else, but if you cannot cope with, say, nouns, at the end of the section about nouns, it would be wise to go back and do something about it.

ORDINARY OF THE MASS

with the Proper of Our Lady for Saturdays and Votive Masses in Advent.

In	nómine	Patris	et	Fílii	et
In	the name	of the Father	and	of the Son	and

Spíritus	Sancti.	Amen
of the Spirit	holy.	

Introíbo	ad	altáre	Dei.
In go will I	to	the altar	of God.

Ad	Deum	qui	laetíficat	juventútem	meam.
To	God	who	joyous makes	youth	my.

---

nomine: *name, nominate, nominal, nomenclature*
Patris: *paternal, patriarch, patristic, patriot, patrimony, patrician, patron*
Filii: *filial, affiliate*
Spiritus: *spiritual, spirit, inspiration*
Sancti: *sanctify, sanctuary, sanctimonious, sanction*
Dei: *Deity, deist*
juventutem: *juvenile, rejuvenate*

6

As you see from the opposite page, you do not have to worry in Latin about the difference between "a" and "the", because Latin leaves them out. It does not tell you whether it is talking about "the altar", or "an altar", or simply "altar".

Latin also frequently leaves out the verb "to be" where English would put it in. We have to translate **Dominus vobiscum,** as "The Lord **be** with you", whereas in Latin, the sense is perfectly clear without the "be".

As you will see from the left-hand pages, most of the Latin words in the Liturgy have English derivatives, so that you can at least make a good guess as to their meaning. The Latin words which you could not possibly recognize from a knowledge of English alone are mostly those responsible for the ordering of the language, such as Prepositions, which order nouns into sentences (from, of, with, into).

PREPOSITIONS, or words "placed before", are also put in front of other words to add to, or modify their meaning. For instance, the Latin originals of: perceive, accept, susceptible, deceive, conceive, are all compounds of one verb (**capere,** to take) with the prepositions meaning: through, to, under, down and together with. So if you know a few important verbs and the prepositions with which they may be compounded, you already possess an extensive Latin vocabulary.

A knowledge of prepositions and their use therefore kills two important birds with one small stone. As prepositions only exist in order to show clearly what a noun is doing in a sentence, we will first consider nouns in connection with prepositions, and then nouns all by themselves.

Júdica	**me,**	**Deus,**	**et**	**discérne**	**causam**	**meam**	**de**
Judge	me,	God,	and	distinguish	cause	my	from

gente		**non**	**sancta:**	**ab**	**hómine**	**iníquo**	**et**	**dolóso**
the people		not	holy:	from	the man	unjust	and	wily

érue	**me.**
away snatch	me.

Quia	**tu**	**es,**	**Deus,**	**fortitúdo**	**mea:**	**quare**	**me**
For	you	are,	God,	strength	my:	why	me

reppulísti,		**et**	**quare**	**tristis**	**incédo**	**dum**
back pushed you,		and	why	sad	walk I	while

afflígit	**me**	**inimícus?**
afflicts	me	the enemy?

Judica: *judge, judiciary*
discerne: *discern*
causam: *cause, causality*
gente: *gentile, gentle, gentleman*
homine: *homicide, homage*
iniquo: *iniquity, equity, equal* (**in,** *here is equivalent to* English **un**)
doloso: *dolose (a legal term meaning "to have criminal intent")*
fortitudo: *fortitude, fortify, fort, force*
reppulisti: *repulse, repel, repulsive*
tristis: *tristful—(an archaic word, but a nice one)*
incedo: *recede*
affligit: *afflict*
inimicus: *inimical, amicable*

PREPOSITIONS

On the opposite page, you see three prepositions:

De, away from, with a sense of up or down from. **De profundis,** From the depths. Romans saw height and depth from a distance, as one vertical line. The word **altus,** "high," also means deep.

Ab, away.

E, or **ex** (prefixed to **rue**), away out of.

The adjectives and nouns following **de** and **ab** have these endings.

sancta   iniquo   gente

doloso   homine

These endings are a result of the action specified by these prepositions. "From" and "away from" show a taking-away action done to the unholy people and the unjust man. So they acquire suitable endings to show what has been done to them.

In other words, these nouns and adjectives are all in the same sort of general situation, or case, which is called the Ablative (**ab,** from, **latus,** carried).

The Ablative Case in general makes a noun do the work of an adverb, to tell you **where, how** or **with what,** something was done. In ancient Latin there were probably three separate cases, whose jobs the Ablative has now taken over. One of these was to show the taking-away kind of action, the second was for the means or instrument with which an action is done, and the third was to show the place where, or time when, something happened. These endings show a general kind of taking-away action, which is made more definite by the prepositions.

Emítte	**lucem**	**tuam**	**et**	**veritátem**	**tuam:**
Forth send	light	Your	and	truth	Your:

ipsa	**me**	**deduxérunt**	**et**	**adduxérunt**
they	me	away have led	and	brought

in	**montem**	**sanctum**	**tuum**	**et**	**in**	**tabernácula**
into	mountain	holy	Your	and	into	tabernacles

tua.
Your.

Et	**introíbo**	**ad**	**altáre**	**Dei,**	**ad**	**Deum**	**qui**
And	I will go in	to	the altar	of God,	to	God	who

laetíficat	**juventútem**	**meam.**
joyous makes	youth	my.

---

emitte: *emit, emissary*
lucem: *lucid, elucidate, Lux* (*the flakes that make clothes Light*)
veritatem: *verity, veracious, verify, veritable, verisimilitude*
deduxerunt: *deduce, deduction*
adduxerunt: *adduce*
montem: *mount, mountain*
tabernacula: *tavern: from an older word "taberna," a hut, hence a little hut or tent*

On the opposite page you see two more prepositions showing motion,

Ad   to

*In   into

The direction of motion is the reverse of that on the previous page, and therefore the nouns which follow **ad,** and **in,** meaning "into", are in a different case, the Accusative, and have a different set of endings.

mont**em**   sanct**um**   tabernacula

tu**um**   tua

De**um**

The Accusative Case shows motion towards. It is also the case of the direct object of the verb, because the object is the thing to which the action of the verb is directed. **Lucem tuam et veritatem tuam** are the objects of the verb **emitte,** and are therefore in the Accusative Case. Its name comes from **ad causam,** "to the cause", and shows that the object of a motion or an action is the final cause of the action.

These two cases, the Ablative and the Accusative, are the only two into which prepositions can put nouns. So far we have these prepositions to show direction or place:

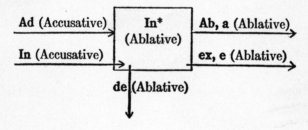

---

* In may also mean "in", as "in the field", and it is then followed by the Ablative Case, to show place where.

11

Confitébor	tibi	in	cíthara,	Deus,	Deus	meus:
Confess will I	to You	on	the cithara,	God,	God	my:

quare	tristis	es,	ánima	mea,	et	quare
why	sad	are you,	soul	mine,	and	why

contúrbas	me?
trouble you	me?

Spera	in	Deo,	quóniam	adhuc	confitébor	illi,
Hope	in	God,	for	even yet	I will confess	to him,

salutáre	vultus	mei,	et	Deus	meus.
the health	of face	my,	and	God	my.

---

confitebor: *confess*
anima: *animate, inanimate*
conturbas: *turbulent, disturb*
spera: *despair*
salutare: *salutation, salute, salutary, salubrious*
cithara: *a musical instrument resembling a harp*

Here are the most important prepositions which put a noun into the Accusative Case. Do not even try to remember them all; notice the possible motions or situations which these prepositions show, and the difference between these and the prepositions which put the noun following into the Ablative Case:

ad: to, into, at, near, according to
adversus: against
ante: before
apud: by, near, in the presence of
circa: about, around, concerning
circum: around
contra: against
inter: among, between

juxta: near
praeter: except, besides, beyond
per: through, by means of
propter: on account of, because of
post: after, behind
secundum: according to
supra: on, upon, above, beyond

And those putting a noun into the Ablative Case:

a, ab, abs: from, by (means, not place—"by force", **not** "by the river")
cum: together with, in company with
de: from, down from, concerning
e, ex: out of, from within
pro: for, on behalf of
prae: before, because of
sine: without
sub: under, below

And those which may "take" either the Accusative or the Ablative, depending on their meaning:

in with Ablative: in, on, at
super with Ablative: concerning, about

in with Accusative: into
super with Accusative: over, on top of, above, beyond

Here is everything you need to know about prepositions. When you meet one in Latin, see if you know what it means, what case follows it, and why. And when you meet them in compounds, notice the effect they have on the meaning of the verb. See if you can find English derivatives containing these prepositions, for instance: ADvent, ANTEroom, INTERpose.

13

n	d		d		d
Glória	**Patri**	**et**	**Fílio**	**et**	**Spirítui**
Glory be	to the Father	and	to the Son	and	to the Spirit

d
Sancto.
Holy.

			ab				
Sicut	**erat**	**in**	**princípio**	**et**	**nunc**	**et**	**semper**
As	it was	in	the beginning	and	now	and	always

		a	g	
et	**in**	**sáecula**	**saeculórum.**	**Amen**
and	into	the ages	of ages.	

---

gloria: *glory*
principio: *principle, principal, prince*
saecula: *secular*

Each noun and adjective in the Latin will henceforth be labelled as to its case. n for Nominative, g for Genitive, d for Dative, a for Accusative, ab for Ablative and v for Vocative. Look at each one and consider why it is in that case.

When you look up a noun in the dictionary, you find both its Nominative and Genitive, as **principium, -i,** (which means that the Nominative is **principium,** the Genitive **principii**) and we will henceforth list all nouns in the vocabulary in this way.

NOUNS AND CASES

There are six different kinds of situations in which a noun may find itself in a sentence.

NOMINATIVE (**nominare,** to name) is the case of the subject, what is being talked about. **Gloria** on the opposite page.

GENITIVE (**genitivus,** of generation or origin) corresponds to the English "of . . ." or "'s". **Dei** = of God, or God's, belonging to God. A noun in the Genitive Case often acts like an adjective and describes another noun by showing its possessor.

VOCATIVE (**vocare,** to call) is used in addressing a person. **Ave, Maria!**

DATIVE (**datus,** given) is the case of the indirect object of an action, that TO, or FOR which something is done. Glory be TO the Father, Gloria **Patri.** "He gave a book to Johnny", **Dedit librum Joanni. Johnny** is the indirect object of the action of giving, **the book** is the direct object. So **Joanni** is in the Dative Case, **librum** in the Accusative.

ACCUSATIVE (**ad causam,** to the cause). The case of the direct object, of motion towards, of extension of time and space. Used after prepositions which give these ideas.

ABLATIVE (**ab + latus,** taken away) used to show place where, time when, means with which, motion from.

In Latin, the Accusative or Ablative Cases may do their work without any prepositions, just as the Dative Case does away with the need for the English "to", or "for" and the Genitive for "of". In the Confiteor, you find **Peccavi cogitatione, verbo et opere.** "I have sinned by thought, by word, and by deed." **Cogitatione, verbo** and **opere,** are all in the Ablative Case, which shows, even with no preposition, that they were the means by which the sinning was done. But prepositions are needed in some cases to make the general meaning of the Ablative or Accusative more specific and definite.

		a	g		a	n
Introíbo	ad	altáre	Dei,	ad	Deum	qui
I will go in	to	the altar	of God,	to	God	who

	a	a
laetíficat	juventútem	meam.
makes joyful	youth	my.

n	n	ab	g	n	
Adjutórium	nostrum	in nómine	Dómini,	qui	fecit
Help	our	in the name	of the Lord,	who	made

a	a
caelum	et terram.
heaven	and earth.

---

adjutorium: *adjutant, coadjutor*
Domini: *dominate, domain, dominion*
caelum: *celestial*
terram: *terrestrial, terrace, terrain*

16

You use cases in speaking or writing English, even if you are unaware of the fact. When you say, "I saw him", you are putting "I" in the Nominative, "him" in the Accusative Case. In Latin almost every noun, pronoun and adjective changes its ending as it changes its case, as our English pronouns change form, and as we add **s** for the plural and **'s** for the Possessive Case.

The advantage of the Latin language is that you can save your word order entirely for emphasis. You do not need it in order to say what you mean. For instance, "The dog bit the man" and "the man bit the dog", use the same words, but mean quite different things. But in Latin, **Canis virum mordet,** or **Virum mordet canis** mean exactly the same thing. The first emphasizes the dog who bit, the second, the man who was bitten.

There is no special virtue in knowing the names of these cases as such. Thousands of people talked Latin quite happily without knowing when they were using the Ablative. But to understand Latin you must know what each case means and how to recognize it, or you will not know what any noun is doing in any sentence.

But there are only these two things to learn about nouns. The most difficult is the one we have been discussing: what the cases mean, so that when you see a noun in the Nominative Case, you know it is the Subject of the sentence or clause, and so on. The second step is much easier—how to recognize the different cases by the endings of the nouns. These two steps will in time become one almost unconscious mental process. You will look at **qui laetificat juventutem meam,** realize that **qui** is in the Nominative Case, **juventutem meam** in the Accusative, and that the meaning therefore is "who makes joyful my youth". And in time, you will not need to advert consciously to the fact that one is "Nominative", the other "Accusative", any more than you consider that "he" becomes "him" in English when it is the object of a verb.

            d   d
Confíteor Deo omnipoténti

d   d   d   d   d   d   d
beátae Maríae semper Vírgini, beáto Michaéli Archángelo, beáto

d   d   d   d   d   d   d
Joánni Baptístae, sanctis Apóstolis Pétro et Páulo, ómnibus

d   d   v
Sanctis et vobis, fratres:

			ab	ab		
quia	peccávi	nimis	cogitatióne,	verbo	et	
That	I have sinned	exceedingly	in thought,	word	and	

ab	ab	ab	ab	ab	ab	ab	ab
ópere,	mea	culpa,	mea	culpa,	mea	máxima	culpa:
deed,	by my	fault,	by my	fault,	by my	greatest	fault:

		a	a		a	a
Ideo	precor	beátam	Maríam	semper	Vírginem,	beátum
Therefore I beseech						

a   a   a   a   a   a
Michaélem Archángelum, beátum Joánnem Baptístam, sanctos

a   a   a   a   a   a   v
Apóstolos Petrum et Paulum, omnes Sanctos, et vos, fratres,

		ab	a	a	a
oráre	pro	me	ad	Dóminum, Deum	nostrum.
to pray	for	me	to	Lord God	our.

	g		n		n
Misereátur	tui	omnípotens	Deus,	et,
May have mercy	on you	all mighty	God,	and,

ab		ab	ab		a
dismíssis	peccátis	tuis	perdúcat	te
having been forgiven	sins	your	through lead	you

a   a
ad vitam aetérnam. Amen
to life   eternal.

---

fratres: *fraternal, fraternity*	**culpa:** *culpable*
peccavi: *impeccable*	**maxima:** *maximum*
cogitatione: *cogitation*	**precor:** *deprecate, imprecation*
verbo: *verb*	**orare:** *oration, oratory, orison*
opere: *operation, operator*	

18

Now that you know in a general way Why Cases, and what each case is used for, the only question is how to recognize from the ending on a noun that it is in a particular case.

On the opposite page, you see that there are three different endings giving **dativeness** to the singular nouns; and three giving **accusativeness** to the same nouns.

Dative:	**ae** (Mariae)	**o** (Petro)	**i** (Virgini)
Accusative:	**am** (Mariam)	**um** (Petrum)	**em** (Virginem)

A list of all the rest of the cases of the noun **Maria,** would look like this:

Nominative:	Maria
Genitive:	Mariae
Dative:	Mariae
Accusative:	Mariam
Ablative:	Maria

You see that there is a part of the word which does not change, **Mari-.** This is called the root and it carries the essential meaning of the word. Immediately after the root, you see the vowel **a,** which, added to the root, forms the stem of the noun, **Maria-.**

Now stems of nouns may end in five main different ways, and according to its stem-ending, a noun is placed in one of five declensions, and takes one of five sets of case-endings. Those nouns whose stem ends in **a,** like **Maria,** are nouns of the First Declension, and take the endings listed above.

A "declension" is so called because the old grammarians considered that a noun had "fallen" from its original pure state when it was not in the Nominative Case. So they named "Cases" as such from the Latin **casus,** meaning a fall. And when you give a list of all the cases of a noun, you "decline" it, or "bend it down" (**de,** down + **clinare,** to bend).

The five declensions were not invented to annoy students. As the language was spoken, different nouns acquired slightly different endings because they sounded more musical. When the grammarians arrived to classify words, they found that there were five main divisions of nouns.

Confíteor Deo omnipoténti beátae Maríae semper Vírgini, beáto Michaéli Archángelo, beáto Joánni Baptístae, sanctis Apóstolis Pétro et Páulo, ómnibus sanctis, et tibi, pater, quía peccávi nimis cogitatióne, verbo et ópere, mea culpa, mea culpa, mea máxima culpa. Ídeo précor beátam Maríam semper Vírginem, beátum Michaélem Archángelum, beátum Joánnem Baptístam, sanctos Apóstolos Petrum et Paulum, omnes sanctos, et te, pater, oráre pro me ad Dóminum, Deum nostrum. Misereátur vestri omnípotens Deus, et, dimíssis peccátis vestris, perdúcat vos ad vitam aetérnam.

a	a		a	g
Indulgéntiam,	absolutiónem	et	remissiónem	peccatórum
Kindness,	absolution	and	remission	of sins

g	d	n		n	n
nostrórum	tríbuat	nobis omnípotens	et	miséricors	Dóminus.
our	grant	to us all powerful	and	merciful	Lord.

NOUNS

1st Declension	2nd	3rd
Maria, Mariae, feminine	Deus, -Dei, masculine	Virgo, Virginis, f.
	Archangelus, -i, m.	Michael, -is, m.
Baptista, Baptistae, m.	Apostolus, -i, m.	Joannes, -is, m.
	verbum, -i, neuter	pater, patris, m.
vita, vitae, f.	Petrus, -i, m.	opus, operis, n.
culpa, culpae, f.	Paulus, -i, m.	absolutio, -onis, f.
indulgentia, -ae, f.	peccatum, -i, n.	remissio, -onis, f.

ADJECTIVES

1st and 2nd	3rd
beatus, beata, beatum	omnis, omne
sanctus, sancta, sanctum	omnipotens, -entis
meus, mea, meum	misericors, -cordis

On the opposite page, some of the nouns and adjectives are listed by declensions. There is no particular reason why the first was called the first, the second the second, and so on, but as this is the way they are usually known, it is easier to learn them in this order.

In regard to those of the first declension, you see that:

The stem ends in **a.**

They are feminine in gender, except **Baptista,** which is obviously masculine.[1]

In regard to the second declension.

The stem-ending is **o,** though you may not believe it. This **o** is the kind of vowel which changes itself into **u** when the accent is not on the syllable, which happens in the Nominative and Accusative Cases. For reasons of its own, it becomes **i** in the Genitive Singular, and the Nominative, Dative and Ablative Plural. But still all second declension nouns have stem ending in **o.**

The nouns in the second declension are either masculine or neuter.[1]

On the opposite page, you see that there are two divisions of adjectives, one coming under the first and second declensions, the other under the third. An adjective needs a masculine, feminine and neuter form so that you can tell what noun it belongs to. So one sort of adjective, like **bonus, bona, bonum,** takes its feminine form from the first declension, its masculine and neuter forms from the second. Such adjectives are listed in dictionaries by giving the masculine, feminine and neuter Nominative forms, because from them you can tell that it is an adjective of the first-and-second declensions, and not one of the third.[2]

AN ADJECTIVE is so named because it is "thrown at" (**ad + jacere,** to throw) a noun, to describe it more fully. It must agree with the noun which it describes in **gender** (masculine, feminine or neuter), **number** (singular or plural) and **case.** And it is said to "modify" its noun (**modus**—manner or mode). For example, **beatae** on the opposite page, is an adjective modifying **Mariae,** which is feminine in gender, singular in number, dative in case. So **beatae** assumes the singular, feminine, dative form.

---

[1] For full declension, see page 165.
[2] For full declension, see page 170.

	v	n	n			a
Deus,	**tu**	**convérsus**		**vivificábis**		**nos**
God,	You	having been turned		will make alive		us

		n	n		ab
et	**plebs**	**tua**	**laetábitur**	**in**	**te.**
And	people	Your	will rejoice	in	You.

	d	v	a	a	
Osténde	**nobis,**	**Dómine,**	**misericórdiam**	**tuam,**	**et**
Show	to us,	O Lord,	mercy	Your,	and

a	a	d	
salutáre	**tuum**	**da**	**nobis.**
salvation	Your	give	to us.

v		a	a		n	n
Dómine,	**exáudi**	**oratiónem**	**meam,**	**et**	**clamor**	**meus**
O Lord,	hear	prayer	my,	and	cry	my

	a	
ad	**te**	**véniat.**
to	You	may it come.

n	ab			ab	ab
Dóminus	**vobíscum.**	**Et**	**cum**	**spíritu**	**tuo.**
The Lord	you with.	End	with	spirit	Your.

---

conversus, -a, -um: *convert, conversion*
plebs, plebis, f: *plebeian, plebiscite*
ostende: *ostensible, ostentation, ostensorium*
miseri-cordia, -ae, f: *miser, miserable, cordial*
exaudi: *audible, audience, audit, audition, auditor*
clamor, clamoris, f: *clamor*
veniat: *advent, prevent, intervene, invent*

If you have looked at the tables of declensions, you will have noticed that the Vocative, or Calling Case, is not included. This is because its case-ending is the same as that of the Nominative. **Ave, Maria!** Maria is in the Vocative Case, but looks exactly the same as the Nominative. The only exception is in the case of nouns of the second declension whose Nominative ends in **us,** such as **Dominus.** Such nouns end in **e** in the Vocative, as **Domine,** which you meet on almost every page of the Liturgy. Now you might think that **Deus,** a noun of the second declension whose Nominative ends in **us,** should follow this rule. But "Dee", did not sound pleasant or right to Latin ears, so it is left as **Deus** in the Vocative too. You do not have to worry about recognizing the Vocative Case when it is the same as the Nominative. It is only the Vocatives ending in **e** that need watching.

The Third Declension is coming on page 27.

FOURTH DECLENSION

The word **spiritus** (**et cum spiritu tuo**) belongs to the Fourth Declension. This, like the second, consists of masculine and neuter nouns. And its stem ends in **u.** This **u** is never lost in any Case, so it is very easy to recognize a fourth-declension noun when you see one. The Holy Name, **Jesus,** belongs to this declension. See page 168.

FIFTH DECLENSION

The words in the Fifth Declension which you will meet most frequently are **dies,** day; **res,** thing; and **fides,** faith. Nouns of the fifth declension are feminine and the stem ends in **e.** See page 169.

SUMMARY

The first declension stem ends in **a,** the Genitive singular in **ae.**

The second declension stem ends in **o,** the Genitive singular ends in **i.**

The fourth declension stem ends in **u,** the Genitive singular ends in **us.**

The fifth declension stem ends in **e,** the Genitive singular ends in **ei.**

Orémus:

		ab		v	a
Aufer	**a**	**nobis,**	**quaésumus,**	**Dómine,**	**iniquitátes**
Away take	from	us,	we ask,	O Lord,	iniquities

a			a	g	ab
nostras,	**ut**	**ad**	**Sancta**	**sanctórum**	**puris**
our,	that	to	the Holies	of Holies	with pure

	ab		a	a
mereámur	**méntibus**	**introíre,**	**per Christum**	**Dóminum**
we may merit	minds	to enter in,	per Christum	Dóminum

a	
nostrum.	**Amen.**

	a	v		a	g
Orámus	**te,**	**Dómine,**	**per**	**mérita**	**Sanctórum**
We pray	you,	Lord,	through	the merits	of Saints

g	g	n			g
tuórum	**quórum**	**relíquiae**	**hic**	**sunt,**	**et**	**ómnium**
Your	whose	relics	here	are,	and	of all

g				a	a
Sanctórum,	**ut**	**indulgére**	**dignéris**	**ómnia**	**peccáta**
the Saints,	that	to pardon	You may deign	all	sins

a	
mea.	**Amen.**
my.	

---

aufer: *infer, defer, refer, prefer, suffer*
quaesumus: *question, quest*
purus, -a, -um: *pure*
mens, mentis, f: *mental, mentality, demented*
meritus, -a, -um: *merit*
reliquia, -ae, f: *relic*
digneris: *deign, dignity*
peccatum, -i, n: *peccadillo, impeccable*

WHAT KIND?

The word "gender", oddly enough, simply means kind or sort, and is akin to "genus", but it is used grammatically to distinguish masculine and feminine and neuter nouns. In English we are very matter of fact, and reserve masculine and feminine gender to persons and to a few other objects which seem to us to have personality, such as pet animals, and ships. In most other languages, this extension of personality went, or goes, much further. French has no neuter gender and all our "its" are divided up into masculine or feminine. Latin has all three genders, but its use of the masculine and feminine is much more extensive than ours. For instance, on the opposite page, 'iniquity' and 'mind' are feminine in gender, but 'merits' and 'sins' are neuter. The gender is a clue to the declension, as you have seen, for the genders are divided among the declensions, like this, with few exceptions:

1ST DECLENSION	2ND DECLENSION	3RD DECLENSION	4TH DECLENSION	5TH DECLENSION
Feminine	Masculine Neuter	Masculine Feminine Neuter	Masculine Neuter	Feminine

You need to know the gender of a noun in order to recognize the adjectives which are modifying it. So note in the vocabulary the gender of each noun while you are considering its declension.

ALL NEUTER nouns, and adjectives, whatever declension they belong to, have:

1. The Nominative and Accusative plural ending in **a**. (On opposite page, sancta, merita, peccata.)
2. The Nominative and Accusative singular are always the same, for instance, **altare** is a neuter noun, so the Accusative singular is **altare** too.

INTROIT

		v		n	
Roráte,	caeli,	désuper,	et	nubes	pluant
Dew,	heavens,	from above,	and	clouds	let rain

a		n		
justum:	aperiátur	terra	et	gérminet
the Just:	opened be	the earth	and	let it bud forth

a		v	a	a
Salvatórem.	Benedixísti,	Dómine,	terram	tuam
a Saviour.	You have blessed,	Lord,	earth	Your,

	a	g	n
avertísti	captivitátem	Jacob.	Glória
you have turned away	the captivity	of Jacob.	

d	d	d	d		ab
Patri et Fílio et Spíritui Sancto, sicut erat in princípio et nunc, et					

	ab	g
semper, et in saécula saeculórum. Amen		

---

caeli, caelorum, m: *celestial*
nubes, nubis, f.
terra, terrae, f: *terrestrial*

Salvator, salvatoris, m: *salvation*
captivitas, captivitatis f: *captivity*
germinet: *germ*
avertisti: (ab + verto, *turn*)
    avert, divert

1	2	3	4
terra	caeli	Salvator	Spiritus
gloria	Dominus	captivitas	
	filius	Pater	
	principium		
	saeculum		

justus, justa, justum
tuus, tua, tuum
sanctus, sancta, sanctum

26

THIRD DECLENSION

Nouns belonging to the third declension do not all have the same stem, but may have any one of four different kinds. Once you know the Nominative and Genitive singular, you are all set for the other cases, but you cannot always tell what the Nominative might be from the Genitive, or vice versa. So when you meet a third declension noun in the vocabulary, pay particular attention to its Nominative and Genitive forms. For instance, the stem of **captivitas,** is **captivitat-,** the final 't' is left out in the Nominative. The stem of **homo** (man) is **homin-,** the stem of **pax** is **pac-,** the 'c' combines with 's' in the Nominative to make **x.** On page 166 you will see the various classifications of these stems, and the declension endings, which are all alike once you get started properly. Do not let all the different possibilities trouble you. After all, if a noun isn't of the 1st, 2nd, 4th or 5th declension, it must be of the 3rd. And nobody will try to make you decline **nubes** if you don't want to.

Adjectives that are not of the first-and-second declension, are of the third. In some, the masculine and feminine forms are exactly alike, and the Neuter only differs in the Nominative and Accusative forms. In the dictionary, the Nominative singular of ⎸the masculine, which is that of the feminine, and the Nominative singular of the Neuter are given. For instance, **omnis, -e** (all) means that **omnis** is the Nominative singular of the masculine and feminine, **omne** of the Neuter (the Genitive of all of them is **omnis**).*

In some others, the forms of all three genders are the same (except for the Neuter Accusative singular which is the same as the Nominative and the Neuter Nominative and Accusative plural which end in **a**). Such adjectives are listed as if they were third declension nouns, giving the Nominative and Genitive singular: **vocans, vocantis** (calling).

In a few third declension adjectives, the Nominative singular is different for the masculine, feminine and neuter, in which case all three are given: **acer, acris, acre** (keen).

---

* See page 171.

Kýrie,	eléison,	Christe,	eléison,	Kýrie,
Lord,	have mercy!	Christ,	have mercy!	Lord,

eléison.*
have mercy!

n		ab	d
Glória	in	excélsis	Deo.
Glory	in	the highests	to God.

		ab	n	d	g	g
Et	in	terra	pax	homínibus	bonae	voluntátis.
And	on	earth	peace	to men	of good	will.

---

gloria, -ae, f.: *glory*
excelsus, -a, -um: *excellent, excel*
terra, terrae, f.
pax, pacis, f.: *peace, Pacific, pacify, pacifist*
homo, hominis, m.: *homicide*
bonus, -a, -um: *bonus*
voluntas, voluntatis, f.: *voluntary, volunteer*

1	2	3
gloria	Deus	pax
terra		homo
		voluntas

excelsis, -a, -um
bonus, -a, -um

---

* The *Kyrie* is in Greek, which you can learn some other time!

Here is one standard example of each of the five declensions all in a row, so that you can compare them and see their similarities and differences.

Singular	1	2	3	4	5
Nominative	gloria	Deus	voluntas	spiritus	dies
Genitive	gloriae	Dei	voluntatis	spiritus	diei
Dative	gloriae	Deo	voluntati	spiritui	diei
Accusative	gloriam	Deum	voluntatem	spiritum	diem
Ablative	gloria	Deo	voluntate	spiritu	die

Plural					
Nominative	gloriae	dei	voluntates	spiritus	dies
Genitive	gloriarum	deorum	voluntatum	spirituum	dierum
Dative	gloriis	deis	voluntatibus	spiritibus	diebus
Accusative	glorias	deos	voluntates	spiritus	dies
Ablative	gloriis	deis	voluntatibus	spiritibus	diebus

The Dative singular ends in a vowel (ae, o, i, i, i,) in all.

The Accusative singular ends in -m (am, um, em, um, em) in all. (This is not necessarily true of neuter nouns, but of all others.)

The Ablative singular ends in a vowel (a, o, e, u, e).

The Genitive plural ends in -um (arum, orum, um, um, um).

The Dative and Ablative plural are the same in each declension.

The Dative and Ablative plural end in -s (is, is, ibus, ibus, ebus). This is the reason why a bus is called a bus, because it was originally an **omnibus,** the Dative plural of the adjective **omnis,** in other words, a "for-all".

The Accusative plural ends in -s (as, os, es, us, us).

In the First Declension, the Nominative and Ablative singular are the same. The Genitive and Dative singular and the Nominative plural are the same.

In the Second Declension, the Genitive singular and Nominative plural are the same. Dative and Ablative singular are the same.

In the Third Declension, the Nominative and Accusative plural are the same.

In the Fourth Declension, the Nominative and Genitive singular, the Nominative and Accusative plural are the same.

In the Fifth Declension, the Nominative singular, Nominative plural and Accusative plural are the same.

	a		a		a
Laudámus	**te,**	**benedícimus**	**te,**	**adorámus**	**te,**
We praise	You,	we bless	You,	we adore	You,

	a
glorificámus	**te.**
we glorify	You.

a		d		a	a
Grátias	**ágimus***	**tibi,**	**propter**	**magnam**	**glóriam**
Thanks	we give	to You,	because of	great	glory

a
tuam.
Your.

---

laudamus: *lauds, laudatory, laudable*
benedicimus: *benediction.* **bene,** *well,* and **dico,** *say*
adoramus: *adore*
glorificamus: *glorify*
gratia, -ae, f.: *grateful, gracious, grace*
***agimus:** *act*
magnus, -a, -um: *magnificent, magnanimous, magnate*

---

* This verb really means: to act, to do, to celebrate. You don't "give" thanks in Latin, you "do" thanks.

SUMMARY

It should be clear by now that the spirit in which to approach Church Latin as a language is that of a self-confident detective, the Sherlock Holmes sort.

Because

There are two things to be learned about any language—Vocabulary and Syntax: In other words—the meanings of words in themselves and how they are related to each other to make sense in sentences.

Church Latin gives practically no vocabulary trouble—there is at least an 80% chance of your knowing the meaning of a word *in itself*.

What you need to learn is how words are related to each other —what significance they have here and now in a sentence.

In English, this additional information is furnished mainly by the order in which the words are given.

In Latin, this information is given mainly by the endings attached to the meaning-carrying part, or stem of the word. We have some of this assistance in English—'s' attached directly to a noun usually makes it plural, ' 's' puts it in the Genitive or Possessive Case—but there is so little of this that English is very difficult to learn. Not so in Latin—every word is doing its best to tell you its significance.

You have seen how this is true of nouns, and a look at the opposite page will show that it is true of verbs too. If you look at **laudamus, benedicimus, adoramus, glorificamus, agimus,** a slight effort will show you that the ending **mus** means "We" do this. Further reflection will convince you that somewhere in those words is given information about the time—present: and about the 'voice'—'we praise', not 'we are praised'. Now in due course, you will be able to gather all this information with one look at a verb, as you are now beginning to gather all the necessary knowledge about a noun, or an adjective. For awhile you will have to follow along like Dr. Watson, but soon you will be your own Sherlock.

31

v	v	v	v	v	v	v
Dómine	Deus,	Rex	caeléstis,	Deus	Pater	omnípotens.
Lord	God,	King	heavenly,	God	Father	all powerful.

v	v	v	v	v	v	v
Dómine	Fili	Unigénite,	Jesu	Christe,	Dómine	Deus,
Lord	Son	only-Begotten,	Jesus	Christ,	Lord	God,

v	g	v	g	n	
Agnus	Dei,	Fílius	Patris,	Qui	tollis
Lamb	of God,	Son	of the Father,	Who	takest away

a	g		d	n	
peccáta	mundi,	miserére	nobis.	Qui	tollis
the sins	of the world,	have mercy	on us.	Who	takest away

a	g		a	a
peccáta	mundi,	súscipe	deprecatiónem	nostram.
the sins	of the world,	receive	prayer	our.

---

rex, regis, m.: *regal, regicide, regalia*
caelestis, -e: *celestial*
mundus, -i, m.: *mundane*
suscipe: *susceptible*
deprecatio, -onis: *deprecate*

2nd Dec.	**3rd Dec.**	**4th Dec.**
dominus, -i, m.	rex, regis, m.	Jesus, -us, m.
deus, -i, m.	pater, patris, m.	
filius, -i, m.	deprecatio, -onis, f.	
Christus, -i, m.		
agnus, -i, m.		
peccatum, -i, n.		
mundus, -i, m.		

1 and 2	**3**
*Unigenitus	caelestis (caeleste, n.)
noster, (nostra, f.; nostrum, n.)	omnipotens

---

* You would never use this in any other connection, so there is no point in giving the feminine or neuter.

32

EXCEPTIONS

As the rules of grammar are merely statements about what has already been done in a language—classifying it, and to some extent regularizing it—there are bound to be exceptions. The forces which govern the formation of languages are gradually being disentangled by philologists—how sounds change, roots develop, words combine—and it is the working of such laws that is responsible for the exceptions, irregular verbs, and so on. The grammarians did their best to make everything tidy, but the living language sometimes would not fit into their pigeonholes. For instance:

If you have been following so far with any degree of interest, you ought to be worried about four words on the opposite page— **Deus, Agnus, Filius** and **Fili,** because these are apparently exceptions to the rule about the Vocative Case. They ought to end in **e,** like **Domine,** since they are Second Declension nouns whose Nominative ends in **us.** If you didn't question how these words got this way, you might go back and read all the pages up to this one over again. If you did worry, you can stop, for there is always some good reason for exceptions.

The first point of language is to convey information, and the second is to convey it in sounds that are pleasing to the ear. This second point is especially important in a Liturgy which any number of people have to say or listen to every day. When the information is sufficiently well conveyed, and the usual rules would make a word difficult to say, or unpleasant in sound, the language disregards the rules. This happens so often in English that there is no infallible guide to English grammar but your "ear"—or someone else's. It doesn't happen so often in Latin, but here it does. **Dee** would sound odd, so they leave it as **Deus. Agne** isn't such a pleasing sound, so it is left as **Agnus. Filie** would sound like **filiae,** the genitive case of **filia,** daughter, so when they want a two-syllable word they have it as **Fili,** and when three syllables sound better, as **Filius.**

33

			a		g	
Qui	**sedes**	**ad**	**déxteram**		**Patris,**	**miserére**
Who	sits	at	the right hand		of the Father,	be merciful

d
nobis.
to us.

	n	n	n	n	n	n
Quóniam	**tu**	**solus**	**sanctus,**	**tu**	**solus**	**Dóminus,**
For	You	alone	holy,	You	alone	Lord,

n	n	n	v	v	ab
Tu	**solus**	**altíssimus,**	**Jesu**	**Christe,**	**cum Sancto**
You	alone	most high,	Jesus	Christ,	with the Holy

ab		ab	g	g	
Spíritu	**in**	**glória**	**Dei**	**Patris.**	**Amen**
Spirit	in	the glory	of God	the Father.	

---

sedes: *sedentary*

dextera, -ae, f.: (*to agree with* **manus, -us,** f., *hand, which is under-stood*) *dextrous, ambidextrous, dexterity*

solus: *sole, solitary, soliloquy, solitaire*

altissimus: *altitude*

1	2	3	4
n	n	n	n
gloria, -ae, f.	Dominus, -i, m.	Pater, Patris, m.	Jesus, -us, m.
	Christus, -i, m.		Spiritus, -us, m.
	Deus, -i, m.		

Adjectives

solus, sola, solum
dexter, dextera, dexterum
sanctus, sancta, sanctum
altissimus, -a, -um

COMPARISON OF ADJECTIVES

An adjective or adverb in any language has three degrees of intensity, as we see by looking at our own adjectives: nice, nicer, nicest; beautiful, more beautiful, most beautiful; good, better, best.

The second of these degrees, which is shown in English by the ending *er* added to the word, or by *more* put in front of it, is called the Comparative, because you expect the word *than* and a comparison to come after it. "Whit*er than* snow". Bett*er than* ever. As we have the ending *er* to show comparison, the Latin adds **ior** to the stem (**altus:** high, **altior:** high*er*) in the masculine and feminine and **ius** in the neuter. Comparatives are declined like third declension adjectives.*

The third of these degrees is called the Superlative (**super:** above, **igtus:** carried), because it takes the noun modified by such an adjective to the top of the class. Corresponding to our *est* ending for the superlative, the Latin usually has **issimus, -a, -um** (as **altissimus,** most high, on the opposite page). Superlatives are declined like second declension adjectives.

Adjectives which end in **-er** in the first or positive degree (**acer:** sharp, **pulcher:** beautiful), add **rimus,** instead of **issimus** to form the superlative (**acerrimus:** sharpest, **pulcherrimus:** most beautiful). And there are a few adjectives which end in **-ilis** (**facilis:** easy), which add **limus** in the superlative (**facillimus:** easiest).

It makes no difference what declension the positive, or simple degree of the adjective is. When it is made comparative, it acquires the ending **ior,** and becomes a third declension adjective. And when it becomes superlative, it acquires the ending **-issimus,** or **-rimus** or **-limus** and becomes a second declension adjective.

You will see on page 172, a list of common adjectives which do not compare regularly. For instance, in English, good, better, best, are not at all alike. In Latin the corresponding words are **bonus, melior, optimus.** The degrees of goodness are different in all languages, because there is a real distinction of quality, besides one of degree, between good and better; better and best.

---

* See page 172.

ORATIO

Orémus: Déus,[v] qui[n] de beátae[g] Maríae[g]
Let us pray: God, Who from of blessed Mary

Vírginis[g] útero[ab] Verbum[a] tuum, Angelo[ab] nuntiánte,[ab]
Virgin the womb, the Word Your, an angel announcing,

carnem[a] suscípere voluísti: praesta supplícibus[d] tuis,[d]
Flesh to take wished, grant to suppliants Your

ut, qui[n] vere eam[a] Genetrícem[a] Dei[g] crédimus,
that, (we) who truly her Mother of God believe,

ejus[g] apud[a] te intercessiónibus[ab] adjuvémur. Per
her with You by intercessions may be helped. Through

eúndem[a] Dóminum[a] nostrum[a] Jesum[a] Christum,[a] Fílium[a]
the same Lord Our Jesus Christ, Son

tuum,[a] qui[n] tecum[ab] vivet et regnat in unitáte[ab] Spíritus[g]
your who with you lives and reigns in unity of the Spirit

Sancti[g] Deus[n] per ómnia[a] sáecula saeculórum.[g] Amen
Holy God through all the ages of ages.

---

beatus, -a, -um: *beatify, beatitude*
virgo, virginis, f.: *virgin*
uterus, -i, m.
verbum, -i, n.: *verb, verbal*
Angelus, -i, m.: *angel*
supplex, -plicis, m.: (sub + plico, *to bend*) *suppliant*
genetrix, genetricis, f.: *generate, generation*
intercessio, intercessionis, f.: *intercession*
unitas, unitatis, f.: *unity*
nuntianti: *announce*
vere: *verily*
credimus: *creed*
regnat: *reign*

36

COMPARISON OF ADVERBS

Adverbs that are formed from adjectives are compared in the same way. From adjectives of the first and second declensions, adverbs are formed by changing the stem vowel, **a** or **o,** to **e.** For instance, **verus, -a, -um,** true, is a first and second declension adjective, and the adverb is **vere,** truly, as you see on the opposite page. From adjectives of the third declension, adverbs are formed by adding **-ter** to the stem. **Mirabilis,** wonderful; **mirabiliter,** wonderfully. So **-e** and **-ter** correspond to our English ending *-ly* which makes an adverb out of an adjective.

The comparative degree of an adverb is the neuter Accusative of the comparative of the corresponding adjective. **Mirabilior, -ius,** is the adjective, therefore **mirabilius** is the adverb (more wonderfully).

The superlative degree is formed in the same way as the positive —by adding **e** to the superlative stem. **Verissimus** (most true) is the adjective, **verissime** (most truly) the adverb.

You now have all the essential material for dealing with nouns, adjectives and adverbs, and all you need is practice in doing so.

This amounts to recognizing what case each noun is in and why.

For the sake of knowing what case: Look at each noun as you meet it in the Latin, see if you know what declension it belongs to, and what gender it is. If you don't know, look down at the vocabulary. When you are expert at this, turn to page 82, where nouns are no longer labelled as to cases. Look at each noun, see if you know its declension and gender and also what case it is in, then and there. The translation is below to help you. When you are expert at this also, turn to page 144 where the translation is quite separate, and do the same thing. If you find it helpful, learn the full declensions of a characteristic noun of each declension, from the tables in the back, and chant them in your bath, or when walking down the street, but such memory-work is useful only if applied to concrete cases. If you do some of this drill before plunging into verbs, you will save yourself a lot of trouble.

Léctio Isaíae Prophétae: Lesson from the Prophet Isaias.

	ab	ab		n		a
In	diébus	illis:	Locútus est	Dóminus	ad	Achaz,
In	days	those,	spoke	the Lord	to	Achaz,

n			a	ab	ab	ab	
dicens:	Pete tibi		signum a	Dómino	Deo	tuo,	in
saying:	Seek for yourself		a sign	from the Lord	God	your,	in

a	g			a		
profúndum	inférni,	sive	in	excélsum	supra.	Et
depths	of hell,	or	in	the height	above.	And

		n				n	
dixit	Achaz:	Non	petam	et	non		tentábo
said	Achaz,	Not	I will seek	and	not		will I tempt

a				v	g
Dóminum.	Et	dixit:	Audíte	ergo,	domus David.
the Lord.	And	he said:	Hear	then,	house of David.

Numquid	n parum	d vobis	est	a moléstos	esse
Not	a little thing	to you	is it	annoying	to be

d		n				d
homínibus,	quia	molésti	estis		et	Deo
to men,	that	annoying	you should be		also	to God

d		a		n	n	d
meo?	Propter	hoc	dabit	Dóminus	ipse	vobis
my?	Because of	this	will give	the Lord	Himself	to you

a	n			g	
signum.	Ecce,	Virgo	concípiet	et	páriet
a sign.	Behold,	a Virgin	shall conceive	and	bear

a		a	n	g	n
Fílium,	et	vocábitur	nomen	ejus	Emmánuel.
a Son,	and	shall be called	name	his	Emmanuel.

a		a			
Butýrum	et	mel	cómedet,	ut	sciat
Butter	and	honey	shall he eat,	that	he may know

a	a		a	
reprobáre	malum	et	elígere	bonum.
to shun	evil	and	choose	good.

---

locutus: *eloquent, locution*   eligere: *eligible, elect*
signum, -i, n.: *sign, signal*   domus, -us, f.: *domicile*
profundus, -a, -um: *profound*   molestus, -a, -um: *molest*
infernus, -i, m.: *infernal*   mel, mellis, n.: *mellifluent*

VERBS

There are four things to be seen in any verb at work in a sentence:

1. WHAT IT MEANS IN ITSELF. You learn this from the root, as in a noun. The root of **tentabo,** I will tempt, is **tent-,** which carries the general idea of tempting. The root of **petam,** I will seek, is **pet-,** giving the general idea of seeking. The root of **audite,** hear, is **aud-,** giving the general idea of hearing.

2. IS IT ACTIVE OR PASSIVE? In other words, is the subject performing the action, or is the action being done to the subject. ('Active' is derived from the verb **agere,** to do; 'passive', from the verb **pati,** to suffer.) The verbs on the opposite page —**pete,** seek; **dixit,** he said; **petam,** I will seek; **tentabo,** I will tempt; **audite,** hear; **dabit,** he will give—are active: but **vocabitur,** will be called, is passive.

    You find this 'voice' of the verb, at the same time as

3. THE PERSON: WHO DID IT? There are only three possibilities:
    The person speaking: I (called in grammar the first person singular). We (first person plural).
    The person spoken to: (Thou) You (second person singular or plural as the case may be).
    A person or thing spoken about: he, she, it (third person singular). They, (third person plural).
    You find this out from the Personal ending.

On the opposite page you see that all the verbs meaning he, (she) did something, **est, dixit, dabit, concipiet, pariet, comedet, sciat,** all end in **-t.** You also see **petam** and **tentabo,** meaning 'I will seek' and 'I will tempt', so you may conclude that the endings **-m,** and **-o,** mean *I* did it.

39

Graduále

	a		v	a				v
Tóllite	**portas,**	**príncipes,**	**véstras:**	**et**	**elevámini,**	**portae**
Lift	gates,	princes,	your,	and	be lifted up,	gates

v		n	g		n
aeternáles,	**et**	**introíbit**	**Rex**	**glóriae.**	**Quis**
eternal,	and	shall go in	the King	of glory.	Who

		a		g		n
ascéndet	**in**	**montem**	**Dómini,**	**aut**	**quis**
shall climb	into	the mountain	of the Lord,	or	who

		ab	ab	g	n	ab
stabit	**in**	**loco**	**sancto**	**ejus?**	**Innocens**	**mánibus**
shall stand	in	place	Holy	His?	The innocent	in hands

	ab	ab		
et	**mundo**	**corde.**	**Allelúia,**	**Allelúia.**
and	of clean	heart.		

	v	ab	v	n	ab
Ave,	**María,**	**grátia**	**plena,**	**Dóminus**	**tecum:**
Hail,	Mary,	with grace	full,	the Lord is	with You,

n	n		ab	
benedícta	**tu**	**in**	**muliéribus.**	**Allelúia.**
blessed	You	among	women.	

---

porta, -ae, f.: *port, portal*
princeps, principis, m.: *prince, principle*
elevamini: *elevator*
rex, regis, m.: *regal*
mons, montis, m.: *Montana, mountain*
locus, -i, m.: *location*
innocens, -entis: *innocent*
manus, -us, f. : *manual*
cor, cordis, n.: *cordial, concord*
plenus, -a, -um: *plenary, plenitude, replenish*

And here is the full list:

voco	I call	ending **o**
vocas	you call	ending **s**
vocat	he calls	ending **t**
vocamus	we call	ending **mus**
vocatis	you call	ending **tis**
vocant	they call	ending **nt**

Etymologists (people who study the origins of words) say that these personal endings are probably fragments of old pronouns, which became added to the verb stem. This theory explains why a pronoun subject (I, he, you, etc.) is contained in the verb. **Voco** means "I call", **vocas** means "you call", without any need for an expressed pronoun.

There is a similar set of endings for the passive. In English we form the passive by using the verb "to be" and a participle. We say: *I am called, he is called.* But Latin does it all with the ending.

vocar	I am called	ending **r**
vocaris	you are called	ending **ris**
vocatur	he is called	ending **tur**
vocamur	we are called	ending **mur**
vocamini	you are called	ending **mini**
vocantur	they are called	ending **ntur**

You see they are quite like the active endings, except in the first person singular and the second person plural.

These are the personal endings in every tense except one. But in the perfect active tense, about which you will hear more later, the personal endings are slightly different. You might as well see them now and know the worst.

vocavi	I have called: I called	ending **i**
vocavisti	you have called: you called	ending **isti**
vocavit	he has called: he called	ending **it**
vocavimus	we have called: we called	ending **imus**
vocavistis	you have called: you called	ending **istis**
vocaverunt	they have called: they called	ending **erunt**

41

          a   a   a   a   v   v
Munda cor **meum** ac lábia mea, **omnípotens Deus,**
Cleanse heart my and lips my, all mighty God,

          a   g   g   ab
qui lábia **Isáiae Prophétae** cálculo **mundásti**
who the lips of Isaias the Prophet with a stone cleansed

  ab
igníto:
burning:

        a   ab   ab   ab
ita me tua **grata miseratióne dignáre mundáre,**
so me by Your free mercy deign to cleanse,

                  a   a   a
ut sanctum **Evangélium tuum digne váleam**
that holy Gospel Your worthily I may be able

                             a   a   a
nuntiáre. **Per Christum Dóminum nostrum.** **Amen**
to announce

---

cor, cordis, n.: *cordial*
labium, labii, n.: *labial*
calculus, calculi, m.: *calculate: (because stones used to be used for counting).*
ignitus, -a, -um: *ignited, ignition*
gratus, -a, -um: *grateful, gratitude*
miseratio, miserationis, f.: *misery, commiseration*
valeam: *valuable, value*
nuntiare: *announce*

42

So far, you know how to find out the Voice and the Person, now we have

4. THE MOOD. The mood (from **modus,** manner) of a verb is like that of a person; how it is feeling. English verbs have moods, but we do not worry about them often. There are four moods.

a. Indicative (from **in + dicare,** to make known) which corresponds to the major mode in musical language. This is the mood used in ordinary talking and speaking. **Mundasti,** on the opposite page, is in the Indicative mood, because it is a simple statement of fact.

b. Imperative (from **imperare,** to command). The use of this is, as in English, to tell or command somebody to do something. **Munda, dignare,** on the opposite page, are both imperatives, as you can tell from the translation. The imperative forms need special personal endings, to differentiate "cleanse!" from a simple "You cleanse"; and, "Be cleansed!" from "You are cleansed". And you will see what these are if you look at the tables on page 178-188.

c. Infinitive (**in** (un) **+ finis,** end or limit), which corresponds to the English 'to' cleanse, 'to' announce. It is called **infinitive** because it does not tell you anything about who did it; the action is not limited to any person. You will see the forms of the infinitive on page 179, but as you see from **mundare** and **nuntiare** on the opposite page, **-re** is the ending of the present active infinitive.

n	s		ab	ab			ab	ab	
Dóminus	sit	in	corde	tuo	et	in	lábiis	tuis,	ut
The Lord	be	in	heart	your	and	on	lips	your,	that

				s		a
digne	et	competénter	annúnties		Evangélium
worthily	and	competently	you may announce	Gospel

a
suum:
His.

ab	g	g	g	g		n
In nómine	Patris	et Fílii et	Spíritus	Sancti.	Amen.	Dóminus

ab	ab	ab
vobíscum.	Et cum	spíritu tuo.

n		g	g		a
Sequéntia		Sancti	Evangélii	secúndum	Lucam.
The continuation	of the Holy	Gospel	according to	Luke.

n	d	v		a	a
Glória	tibi	Dómine!	Per	evangélica	dicta
Glory	to You,	Lord!	Through	the evangelic	words

s		a	a
deleántur		nostra	delícta.
blotted out be	our	sins.

---

competenter: *competently*
annunties: *announce*
sequentia, -ae, f.: *sequence*
dictus, -a, -um: *dictate, diction*
deleantur: *delete*
delictus, -a, -um: *delict*

44

d. Subjunctive (from **sub** + **iungere,** to join) is the only one of the grammatical moods to merit the name of mood in our sense of the word. It is called the Subjunctive, because verbs in clauses which are "joined under" the main verb, are sometimes in the Subjunctive. It is not a good name, because verbs in clauses may be in the Indicative mood, and because the Subjunctive may be the mood of the main verb anyway. Moreover, its name gives you no idea of the quality of the mood.

We have the Subjunctive in English, and strictly speaking, we ought to use it more than we do. When you say, "I wish it was a fine day", if you have ever had a course in English grammar, you probably have a vague feeling that you should have said, "I wish it were a fine day." 'Were' used this way is our Subjunctive form of the verb 'to be'. Our English 'may' is another rendition of the subjunctive. "May the Lord be in your heart!" In general, the subjunctive is used to express wishes, hopes, purposes—and not straight statements or commands. As Latin uses the subjunctive mood more consciously than does English, and as there is no one translation for it, the first step in recognizing it is to realize how a Roman felt when he used this mood. The second step is to be able to recognize the Subjunctive when you see it so that you can feel the same way.

To facilitate these two steps, we will label each verb in the Latin henceforth as to its mood. i, for Indicative, imp. for Imperative, inf. for Infinitive and s for Subjunctive.

45

	ab	ab		i	n	n	
In illo	**témpore:**	**Missus**	**est**	**Angelus**	**Gábriel**	**a**
At that	time:	Sent	was	the Angel	Gabriel	from

	ab		a	g	d	n	n
Deo	**in**	**civitátem**	**Galilaéae,**	**cui**	**nomen**	**Názareth,**
God	into	a city	of Galilee,	whose	name	Nazareth,

	a		a	d	d	n	i
ad	**Vírginem**	**desponsátam**	**viro,**	**cui**	**nomen**	**erat**
to	a Virgin	espoused	to a man,	whose	name	was

n		ab		g		n
Joseph,	**de**	**domo**	**David,**	**et**	**nomen**
Joseph	of	the house	of David,	and	the name

g		n	n	n
Vírginis	**María.**	**Et**	**ingréssus**	**Angelus**	**ad**
of the Virgin	Mary.	And	having come in	the Angel	to

a	i	imp.	ab	v̆	n
eam,	**dixit:**	**Ave,**	**grátia**	**plena,**	**Dóminus**
her,	said:	Hail,	with grace	full,	the Lord

ab	n	n		ab
tecum,	**benedícta**	**tu**	**in**	**muliéribus.**
is with you,	blessed	you	among	women.

---

tempus, -oris, n.: *temporal*
missus: *mission*
civitas, -atis, f.: *civil*
vir, viri, m.: *virile, virtue*

46

But you can recognize a mood from the form of the verb, and you do this when you are finding out its

5. TENSE, OR TIME—(**tempus,** time), in other words, when the action took place.

In English or Latin, the main divisions of time are Present, Past and Future, and each of these may be subdivided to tell you whether the action is continuing, or is all finished. Latin has fewer possible tenses than English, as they were not so particular about distinguishing a continuing action (I am walking) from a simple one (I walk), which does not tell you whether the action is continuing, or not. Here are all the Latin tenses, with their English equivalents.

Present		**amo**	I love, I am loving
(Past)	*Imperfect*	**amabam**	I was loving
	Perfect	**amavi**	I loved, I have loved
	Pluperfect	**amaveram**	I had loved
Future		**amabo**	I shall love, I shall be loving
Future Perfect		**amavero**	I shall have loved

As you see, the Present, the Future and the Perfect have two English equivalents, but the sense of the sentence will tell you which one is meant. For instance, on the opposite page, **dixit** is in the perfect tense, and obviously means 'he said', rather than 'he has said'.

When you look at these various tenses of **amo,** you see that the part of the verb that tells its time comes between the stem and the personal ending: ama - **ba** - m , ama - **v** - i , ama - **b** - o. If you look at the tables on pages 178-188 you will see what these signs are for all verbs, but first we must consider the four conjugations, which correspond to the five declensions of nouns.

a   s   n   i

Quae   **cum**   **audísset,**   **turbáta**   **est**   **in**
Which things   when   she had heard,   troubled   she was   at

ab   g   i   n   s   n

sermóne **ejus,** **et**   **cogitábat**   **qualis**   **esset**   **ista**
word   his,   and   was thinking   what kind   was   this

n   i   n   d   s

salutátio. **Et**   **ait**   **Angelus**   **ei:**   **Ne**   **tímeas,**
greeting.   And   said   the Angel   to her: Not   fear,

v   i   a   a

María,   **invenísti**   **enim**   **grátiam**   **apud**   **Deum.**
Mary,   you have found   for   grace   with   God.

imp.   i   ab   i   a

Ecce   **concípies**   **in** **útero**   **et**   **páries** **Fílium,**
Behold   you will conceive   in   the womb   and   bear   a Son,

i   a   g   a

et   **vocábis**   **nomen**   **ejus** **Jesum.**
and   you will call   name   His   Jesus.

                                       Infinitive

audisset: *audition*   audire—4th conjugation
turbatus, -a, -um: *perturb, disturb*
sermo, sermonis, m.: *sermon*
cogitabat: *cogitation*   cogitáre—1st
qualis, -e: *quality*
salutatio, -onis, f.: *salutation*
timeas: *timid, intimidate*   timére—2nd
invenisti: *invent*
concipies: *conception, conceive*   concípĕre—3rd
vocabis: *vocal, vocation*   vocáre—1st

Though the personal endings remain the same for every verb, the letters in the word vary which give you the information as to Mood and Tense. As there are five declensions of nouns, so there are four conjugations or joinings-together (con + iungere, to join) of verbs. And as a noun belongs to its declension because of its stem, so a verb belongs to its conjugation because of its stem. The stem is the root, with an additional vowel which is the sign of the conjugation to which the verb belongs. For instance in the word **cogitabit** on the opposite page:

cogit- is the root, which carries the idea of thinking.

cogita- is the stem: the root + the vowel **a,** which shows that the verb belongs to the first conjugation.

cogitaba- is the stem + the sign of the imperfect tense, **ba.**

cogitabat is the completed verb in action with the personal ending **-t.**

a is the stem vowel of the first conjugation.

e is the stem vowel of the second. This **e** is long and pronounced like the **a** in 'fate'.

e is the stem vowel of the third. This **e** is short, like the **e** in 'let'.

i is the stem vowel of the fourth, pronounced as in 'machine'.

On the opposite page, **cogitáre** is of the first; **timére** is of the second; **concípere** is of the third; **audíre** is of the fourth conjugation.

(When you are talking about a verb, you usually use the present active infinitive form, as we do in English when talking about the verb *to think.*)

Remember that all this analysis of verbs and how they are conjugated, or put together, was done after the actual words had been in use for centuries. All the various forms are the result of an age-long process of addition. For instance, it is probable that the tense sign for the imperfect tense (**ba**) was originally a part of the verb 'to be', used in the same way as our 'was'. 'I was calling'. If you reversed this to 'calling-was-I' and then made it into one word, 'callingwasI', which becomes in the course of time 'callisi', you have an analogy of the process by which scholars think that the various forms of verbs were brought into the language.

n	i	n		n	g
Hic	**erit**	**magnus**	**et**	**Fílius**	**Altíssimi**
He	shall be	great	and	the Son	of the Highest

i		i	d	n	n
vocábitur,	**et**	**dábit**	**illi**	**Dóminus**	**Déus**
shall be called,	and	will give	to Him	Lord	God

a	g	g	g		i	
sedem	**David,**	**pátris**	**ejus,**	**et**	**regnábit**	**in**
the seat	of David,	father	His,	and	he shall rule	in

ab	g		a	g	g
domo	**Jacob**	**in**	**aetérnum,**	**et**	**regni**	**ejus**
the house	of Jacob	into	eternity,	and	of kingdom	His

	i	n
non	**erit**	**finis.**
not	shall be	end.

i		n		a	ab	ab
Dixit	**autem**	**María**	**ad**	**Angelum:**	**Quo**	**modo**
Said	but	Mary	to	the Angel:	By what	means

		n		a		i	
fiet	**istud,**	**quóniam**	**virum**	**non**	**cognósco?**	**Et**
shall be done	this,	for	man	not	know I?	And

n	n	i	d	n	n
respóndens	**Angelus,**	**dixit**	**ei:**	**Spíritus**	**Sanctus**
answering	the Angel,	said	to her:	Spirit	Holy

i		ab	n	g
supervéniet	**in**	**te,**	**et**	**virtus**	**Altíssimi**
shall come down	upon	you,	and	the power	of the Highest

i	d
obumbrábit	**tibi.**
shall overshadow	you.

---

sedes, sedis, f.: *sedentary*
regnum, -i, n.: *reign, interregnum*
finis, finis, m.: *finish*
cognosco: *cognition, cognizant*
respondens: *respond*
virtus, virtutis, f.: *virtue*

Infinitive
cognoscĕre—3rd
respondĕre—2nd

50

Now you would have all the information you need in order to find out the entire meaning of any verb, if all verbs were absolutely 'regular' (**regula,** rule). You know the personal endings, from which you tell the **Person** and **Voice.** When you have studied the tables of verbs for a short time, you will be able to recognize also the signs of tense and mood, and as soon as you see the characteristic conjugation-vowel, you know which of the tense-and-mood signs apply.

But there are any number of verbs which are not entirely regular, and these are apt to be the words used most frequently. But all of them form their various moods and tenses "regularly" from certain main "stems", or principal parts, so that, if you know each of these main possible forms of a verb, you can tell what the rest are. For instance, in English, if you want to use the verb *to give* in general conversation, you need to know *give, gave* and *given.* Once you know these you can use the word in any possible situation. In other words you need to know:

> the present infinitive: to give
> the first person of the past: I gave
> the past passive participle: given

In the same way in Latin, once you know its "principal parts" you can deal with any verb freely and fluently.

These principal parts are:

voco (I call)   the first person singular of the present indicative
vocare (to call) the present active infinitive
vocavi (I called) the first person singular of the perfect active
vocatus (called) the perfect passive participle*

Henceforth you will find all verbs in the vocabulary given with their principal parts. As **voco, vocare, vocavi, vocatus,** or in abbreviation, **voco, -are, -avi, -atus.** But when the principal parts are not regular, you will find each written out, as **do, dare, dedi, datus.**

------
* See footnote, page 197.

51

			n	i		ab	a
Ideóque	et	quod	nascétur		ex	te	Sanctum
Therefore	also	what	shall be born		of	you,	the Holy One,

		i		n	g		imp.	n
vocábitur		Fílius		Dei.	Et	ecce,	Elízabeth,
shall be called		the Son		of God.	And	behold	Elizabeth,

n	n		n	i		a		ab
cognáta	tua,	et	ipsa	concépit		fílium	in	senectúte
cousin	your,	also	she	has conceived		a son	in	old age

ab		n	n	n	i	d		n	i
sua,	et	hic	mensis	sextus	est	illi,		quae	vocátur
her,	and	this	month	sixth	is	to her,		which	is called

n			i		n		a
stérilis,	quia	non	erit		impossíbile	apud	Deum
barren,	for	not	shall be		impossible	with	God

n	n		i		n	imp.		n
omne	verbum.	Dixit	autem	María:	Ecce		ancílla
any	word.	Said	then	Mary:	Behold		the handmaid

g		s		d		a	a
Dómini,	fiat		mihi	secúndum		verbum	tuum.
of the Lord,	be it done		to me	according to		word	your.

---

voco, vocare, vocavi, vocatus: *vocative, voice*

concipio, -cipere, -cepi, -ceptus: *conception*

sum, esse, fui, futurus: (*This is the future participle—you can't have a passive participle of the verb 'to be'. Just try!*)

dico, dicere, dixi, dictus: *diction*

Verbs have no past participle when they are "intransitive", that is when the action cannot go across (**trans**) to an object. Such verbs cannot have any passive voice. For instance, you could not say, "I was trembled"—so the verb **tremere** has no passive participle and only three principal parts.

Now this is the way the various tenses and moods are formed from these principal parts. (Only for people who like diagrams.)

From the first two principal parts, you find the present stem, in this case **voca-** from which are formed:

Indicative

	Active		Passive	
Present	**voco**	I call	**vocor**	I am called
Imperfect	**vocabam**	I was calling	**vocabar**	I was being called
Future	**vocabo**	I shall call	**vocabor**	I shall be called

Subjunctive

Present	**vocem**		**vocer**	
Imperfect	**vocarem**		**vocarer**	

Imperative

Present	**voca**	call!	**vocare**	Be called
Future	**vocato**		**vocator**	

Infinitive

Present	**vocare**	to call	**vocari**	To be called

Participle

Present	**vocans**	calling	*Gerundive* **vocandus**	
Gerund	**vocandi**	of calling		

Perfect stem **vocav-** (from **vocavi**)　　*Supine stem* **vocat-** (from **vocatus**)

Indicative

Perfect	**vocavi**	I called	**vocatus sum**	I was called
Pluperf.	**vocaveram**	I had called	**vocatus eram**	I had been called
Fut. Perf.	**vocavero**	I shall have called	**vocatus ero**	I shall have been called

Subjunctive

Perfect	**vocaverim**		**vocatus sim**
Pluperf.	**vocavissem**		**vocatus essem**

Infinitive

Perfect	**vocavisse**	to have called	

Supine stem **vocat-**

Infinitive

Perfect			**vocatus esse**
Future	**vocaturus esse**		**vocatum iri**

Participle

Future	**vocaturus**		*Perfect* **vocatus**
Supine	**vocatum, vocatu**		

i	a	a	a	a
Credo	**in**	**unum**	**Deum,**	**Patrem**	**omnipoténtem,**
I believe	in	one	God,	the Father	all mighty,

a	g		g	g		g
factórem	**caeli**	**et**	**terrae,**	**visibílium**		**ómnium**
maker	of heaven	and	earth,	of visible things	all

	g		a	a	a
et	**invisibílium.**	**Et**	**in**	**unum**	**Dóminum,**	**Jesum**
and	of invisible.	And	in	one	Lord,	Jesus

a	a	g	a		
Christum,	**Fílium**	**Dei**	**unigénitum.**	**Et**	**ex**
Christ,	Son	of God	only-begotten.	And	from

ab	a		a	a	a	
Patre	**natum**	**ante**	**ómnia**	**sáecula;**	**Deum**	**de**
the Father	born	before	all	ages.	God	of

ab	a		ab	a	a	ab	ab
Deo,	**lumen**	**de**	**lúmine,**	**Deum**	**verum**	**de**	**Deo**	**vero,**
God,	light	of	light,	God	true	of	God	true,

a		a	a	g
génitum	**non**	**factum,**	**consubstantiálem**	**Patri,**
begotten	not	made,	consubstantial	with the Father,

	a	a		i
per	**quem**	**ómnia**	**facta**	**sunt.**
through	whom	all things	made	were.

---

credo, -ere, crédidi, creditus: *creed*
unus, -a, -um: *unite*
factor, factoris, m.: *fact, factor, manufacture*
natus, -a, -um: *natal, nativity*
lumen, luminis, n.: *luminous, illumine*
verus, -a, -um: *veracity, verily*
gigno, -ere, genui, genitus: *generator*
facio, facere, feci, factus: *fact, factor*
consubstantialis, -e: (con + sub + sto)

If you were trying to learn Latin so that you could write it yourself, you really would need to know this table so that you could make out one of your own for every Latin verb. But for our purposes, it is sufficient to have a general idea of the scheme. To do this, you see that you need to become well acquainted with the verb **esse,** to be, because you use it in forming all the past passive tenses. A verb used in this way, as we use both 'to have' and 'to be' in English (I have said, I was walking) is called an auxiliary, or helping verb.

If you look at page 176, you will see all the forms of the verb **esse,** and, whatever else you may omit, you had better take a good look at them.

On that summary of forms, which is called a synopsis (from the Greek **syn,** together, **opsis,** see), you may have noticed four participles.

A participle is a verb used as an adjective. On the opposite page, 'born', 'begotten'. It gets its name because it participates, or shares in the nature both of a verb and of an adjective.

As a verb, it expresses action, and may have an object. 'Seeing a ship, he shouted.' *'Seeing'* is a present participle, and *'ship'* is its object.

As an adjective, it modifies a noun, and agrees with it in gender, number and case. **Natum, genitum, factum** all agree with their noun, **Jesum Christum.** Latin writers, especially of ecclesiastical Latin, used participles much more freely than we do in English, as you will see.

A Latin verb has four participles:

1. Present active participle, corresponding to our English 'calling', 'hearing'. And the ending is the conjugation vowel + **ns.** The present participle of the verb **vocare** is **vocans,** of **timere** is **timens.** Present participles are declined like third declension adjectives, so that the Genitive singular is **vocantis, timentis.**

Omnipotentem, on the opposite page is an adjective developed from the present participle of the verb **possum,** meaning "to be able". Its present participle is **potens, -entis.** Many of our English adjectives ending in -ent, or -ant, such as omnipotent, beneficent, are derived from Latin present participles.

55

n   a   a   a
Qui propter nos hómines, et propter nostram
Who because of us men, and because of our

 a   i   ab
salútem, descéndit de caelis. Et incarnátus
salvation, descended from the heavens. And incarnate

 i   ab   ab   ab ab
est de Spíritu Sancto, ex María Vírgine, et
was of the Spirit Holy, from Mary Virgin, and

 n   i   d
homo factus est. Crucifíxus étiam pro nobis sub
man made was. Crucified also for us under

 ab   ab   i
Póntio Piláto, passus et sepúltus est. Et
Pontius Pilate, suffered and buried was. And

 i   ab ab   a
resurréxit tértia die, secúndum Scriptúras. Et
He rose the third day, according to the Scriptures. And

 i   a   i   a
ascéndit in caelum: sedet ad déxteram
He ascended into Heaven, sits at the right hand

 g   i   ab
Patris. Et íterum ventúrus est cum glória,
of the Father. And again to come He is with glory,

 inf.   a   a   g   g
judicáre vivos et mórtuos. Cujus regni non
to judge the living and the dead. Of whose kingdom no

 i   n
erit finis.
shall be end.

---

salus, salutis, f.: *salute, saluta-*
 tion, salutary
descendo, -ere, descendi, des-
 census: *descend*
patior, pati, passus: *passion,*
 passive
sepultus, -a, -um: *sepulchre*
tertius, -a, -um: *tertiary, Terce*
ascendo -ere, -endi, -ensus: *as-*
 cend

iterum: *iterate*
judico, -are, -avi, -atus: *judicial,*
 adjudicate
vivus, -a, -um: *vivid, vivify, revive*
morior, mori, mortuus: *mortu-*
 ary, mortify, 'mortician'
regnum, regni, n.: *reign, inter-*
 regnum
finis: *finish, infinite*

2. Perfect Passive Participle, corresponding to the English one ending in **ed,** 'called', 'loved', 'feared'. As this is the last principal part of a verb, you know what it is if you know the principal parts. On the opposite page, you see **factus, crucifixus, passus, sepultus**—all past participles. They are first and second declension adjectives, like **bonus, bona, bonum. Mortuos** is a past participle used as a noun: *the dead,* or *those who have died.*

3. Future Active Participles, of which **venturus** is an example. **Venturus est** is translated as 'He is about to come', but 'He is going to come' expresses the idea more closely and colloquially. The future participle is used to express what is likely or about to happen. When it is used as it is here, with the verb **to be** it forms what is called a **periphrastic** conjugation. 'Periphrastic' simply means a round-about way of saying something.

4. Gerundive. We will tell you about this participle later—you will not meet one for a long time.

If you look at the principal parts of **patior,** suffer, given on the opposite page, you see that there are only three of them, and they do not look like the principal parts of an ordinary verb, like **adoro, -are, -avi, -atus.** The first part, **patior,** is the first person singular of the present *passive*, the second is the *passive* infinitive, there is no perfect active, and the last is, as usual, the perfect *passive* participle. Such verbs are passive in form, but they have an active meaning. They are called deponent, or 'down-placing' verbs.

Such verbs are really neither active nor passive in meaning. They are 'middle voice': That is, they represent the subject as acting *upon* himself or *for* himself. Consider our use of the verb *to enjoy* in the sentence: "I enjoyed myself at the theatre." Obviously I did not enjoy *myself*; I took enjoyment *for* myself. But the 'middle' meanings of these deponent verbs are lost to us, so we translate them as actives.

There are a few verbs which are semi-deponent, that is, have active forms in the present and future tenses, and only passive in the past. But you can tell what these are from their principal parts.

    a   a   a   a

Et   **in**   **Spíritum**   **Sanctum,**   **Dóminum et**   **vivificántem**
And   in   the Spirit   Holy,   the Lord   and   living-maker;

n   ab   ab   i   n

Qui   **ex**   **Patre**   **Filióque**   **procédit.**   **Qui**   **cum**
Who   from   the Father   and the Son   proceeds,   Who   with

ab   ab   i

Patre   **et**   **Fílio**   **simul**   **adorátur**   **et**
the Father   and   the Son   together   is adored   and

        i   n   i   a

conglorificátur,   **Qui**   **locútus est**   **per**   **prophétas.**   **Et**
glorified,   Who   spoke   through   the prophets.   And

 a   a   a   a   a

unam   **sanctam,**   **cathólicam**   **et**   **apostólicam**   **Ecclésiam.**
one   holy,   catholic   and   apostolic   Church.

   i   a   a   a   g

Confíteor   **unum**   **baptísma**   **in**   **remissiónem**   **peccatórum.**
I confess   one   baptism   into   remission   of sins.

        i   a   g   a

Et   **exspécto**   **resurrectiónem**   **mortuórum**   **et**   **vitam**
And   expect   the rising again   of the dead,   and   life

g   g

ventúri   **sáeculi.**   **Amen**
of the coming   world.

---

vivifico, -are, -avi, -atus: *vivify*
procedo, procedere, processi, processus: *proceed*
simul: *simultaneous*
adoro, adorare, adoravi, adoratus: *adore*
conglorifico, -ficare, -ficavi, ficatus: *glorify*
loquor, loqui, locutus: *eloquent*
ecclesia, ecclesiae, f.: *ecclesiastical*
confiteor, confiteri, confessus: *confess*
remissio, remissionis, f.: *remission, remit*
exspecto, -spectare, -spectavi, -spectatus: *expect (compounded from* **ex** *and* **specto,** *to look, so its original and vivid meaning is to look out for)*

SUMMARY

After all this information, here is a summary of what you really need to know about verbs.

1. THE PERSONAL ENDINGS, ACTIVE AND PASSIVE—the same for all verbs.
2. SIGNS OF TENSE AND MOOD—varying slightly for each conjugation.
3. PRINCIPAL PARTS.
4. The verb **esse**, to be, in all its forms.

You will find that it is a good idea to study the tables of regular verbs.* But, after a little of such study, take each verb that you meet in the Latin text, look at its principal parts, as listed below, and ask yourself its person, mood and tense. If you do not know, look it up in the tables.

This process may sound tedious, but it uses almost the same part of your mind as the working out of an easy cross-word puzzle. And when you have done enough of it so that it becomes an almost unconscious mental process, you will get more satisfaction than you do from solving any possible made-up puzzle.

---

* See pages 178-188.

    n   ab   ab   ab   s   imp.   v
Dóminus vobíscum. Et cum spíritu tuo. Orémus: Ave, María,

  ab   v   n   ab   n   n   ab
grátia plena; Dóminus tecum: benedícta tu   in   muliéribus
                             blessed   you among women

        n   n   g   g
et   benedíctus fructus ventris tui.
and blessed   the fruit of womb your.

  imp.   v   v   v   v   v   a
Súscipe, sancte Pater,   omnípotens aetérne Deus, hanc
Receive, holy Father, almighty   eternal God, this

  a   a   a   n   n   n
immaculátam hóstiam, quam ego, indígnus fámulus
immaculate victim,   which I,   unworthy servant

  n   i   d   d   d   d   d
tuus, óffero tibi,   Deo meo vivo et   vero, pro
Your, offer to You, God my living and true, for

    ab   ab   ab
innumerabílibus   peccátis   et   offensiónibus   et
innumerable   sins   and   offenses   and

    ab   ab
neglegéntiis meis,
negligences my,

---

oro, -are, -avi, -atus: *oratory*
suscipio, -cipere, -cepi, -ceptus (sub + capio): *susceptible*

You are often told in courses on How to Write that you should always use words of Anglo-Saxon rather than of Latin origin. The reason is that we still feel something of the concrete derivations of Anglo-Saxon words, but not of Latin, so such words are abstract and colorless. For instance, to us, the word 'negligence' only means something not done that should have been done. But the Roman felt the force of its two compounding words—**neg,** not, **legere,** to pick up. The word **neglegentia** conveyed the concrete notion of something not picked up, as well as its abstract meaning.

This verb **legere** shows what can happen to a word and its compounds. Its original meaning was 'to pick up', 'to gather together'. **Neglegere** is an offshoot of this meaning. So is **colligere** (**con + legere**) 'to collect', which is its English derivative.

Legere then acquired the meaning of 'to choose', which is shown in its compounds: **seligere,** from which we get 'select'; **eligere (ex + legere)** from which we get 'elect' and 'eligible'; **diligere (de + legere),** which literally means 'to choose away from', but acquired the meaning of 'to love', 'to esteem'. From the present participle of this verb, **diligens,** we get our words 'diligent', 'diligence'. And the past participle, **dilectus,** means 'chosen', 'beloved'. At the Baptism of Our Lord, a voice was heard saying, **"Hic est Filius meus dilectus."** We have a further compound of this in English, **pre + de + lectus**—'predilection'.

But **legere** acquired another meaning, 'to read', because in early writing there were no spaces between words, and in reading you had to 'pick out' the letters of each word. When you meet **legere** by itself with no prefixes, it usually means 'to read'. From this we get 'legible' and its opposite 'illegible'. And finally there is **intellegere (inter + legere)** 'to read into', or 'to understand', from which we get 'intellect', 'intelligent'.

		ab	ab		sed	et	pro
et	pro	ómnibus	circumstántibus,		sed	et	pro
and	for	all	those standing around,		and	also	for

	ab	ab	ab	ab		ab
ómnibus	fidélibus	christiánis,	vivis	atque	defúnctis,
all	faithful	Christians,	living	and	dead,

d		d	s		a	
ut	mihi	et	illis	profíciat	ad	salútem	in
that	me	and	them	it may profit	to	salvation	into

a	a	
vitam	aetérnam.	Amen
life	eternal.	

---

circumsto, -stare, -steti, -status: *circumstance*
proficio, -ere, -feci, -fectus (pro + facio): *proficient*
fidelis, -e: *confide, fidelity*
salus, salutis, f.: *salutary*

From all this, you see that it is useful to know the principal parts of the most used Latin verbs, since the English derivatives may come from any of them, and a knowledge of such main verbs and their compounds will go far to revivify a large part of the English language.

Here are some of the Latin possibilities of the verb **facio,** to make. See how many English derivatives you can find from each. Its Principal Parts are: **facio, facere, feci, factus.**

ad: afficere to do something to, influence, affect, also punish
ob: officere to hinder, obstruct
con: conficere bring together, produce, complete
inter: interficere kill
per: perficere carry out, perform, complete
prae: praeficere place in authority, appoint
in: inficere infect, instruct, dye
de: deficere abandon, fail
e (ex): efficere accomplish
sub: sufficere supply, satisfy
pro: proficere make for, succeed, perform, help, profit
re: reficere restore, rebuild

Facere turns into a first conjugation verb when combined with nouns or adjectives.

sacer: sacrifico, -ficare, -ficavi, ficatus
sanctus: sanctifico
vivus: vivifico
aedus (temple): **aedifico**
laetus: laetifico
gloria: glorifico
pax: pacifico

v	n	g	g	a	
Deus,	**qui**	**humánae**	**substántiae**	**dignitátem**	**mirabíliter**
God,	Who	of human	substance	the dignity	wonderfully

i				i	imp	d
condidísti	**et**	**mirabílius**		**reformásti,**	**da**	**nobis**
built	And	more wonderfully		reformed,	give	us

	g	g		g	a	g
per	**hujus**	**aquae**	**et**	**vini**	**mystérium,**	**ejus**
through	of this	water	and	wine	the mystery,	of His

g	inf.	a	n	g	g
divinitátis	**esse**	**consórtes,**	**qui**	**humanitátis**	**nostrae**
divinity	to be	sharers	who	of humanity	our

inf	i	n	n	n
fíeri	**dignátus est**	**párticeps,**	**Jesus Christus,**	**Filius tuus,**
to be made	deigned	partaker,		

n	n	n	abl.	i		i	abl.
Dóminus	**noster,**	**Qui**	**tecum**	**vivit**	**et**	**regnat**	**in**	**unitáte**

g	g	n	a	a	g
Spíritus	**Sancti**	**Deus,**	**per ómnia**	**sáecula**	**saeculórum.**	**Amen**

---

humanus, -a, -um: *human*
substantia, -iae, f.: *substance*
mirabiliter: *admirable*
condo, condere, condidi, conditus: *condition*
reformo, -formare, -formavi, -formatus: *reform*
fio, fieri, factus sum: (*passive of* **facere**, see page 189)
aqua, aquae, f.: *aquamarine, aqueous, aquarium*
vinum, vini, n.: *vine, wine, vintage*
mysterium, mysterii, n.: *mystery*
consors, consortis, m.: *consort*
humanitas, -tatis, f.: *humanity*
particeps, -cipis, m.: *participate*
regno, regnare, regnavi, regnatus: *reign*

From most of those verb compounds of **facio,** corresponding adjectives, adverbs and nouns have been made. For instance, from **facio** itself:

facilis, easy, **facile,** easily, **facilitas,** easiness, facility
factum, that which has been done, a deed, **factus,** worked, wrought, (from the past participle)
facultas, ability, faculty
factio, a making, doing, **factiosus,** fond of power
and you can see what the English derivatives are.

So it is obvious that if you know: 1. the root verb, 2. its principal parts and 3. the prepositions, etc., with which compounds are made, the chances are that you will be able to make a good guess as to what the compound means, especially with an English derivative to help you.

But sometimes the meaning will have acquired a twist which you could not know about unless you looked it up.

The advantage of this way of looking at words is that you find out what they really mean—in English or Latin.

reformare actually means to re-form, to refashion.
sub-stantia: that which stands under—a substance.
con-sors: con, together + **sors,** lot, so 'consorts' are those who share the same lot. Similarly 'companions' comes from **com +
panis,** bread—those who eat bread together.
particeps: pars + capio, literally a part-taker.

	i	d	v	a	g	a
Offérimus	**tibi,**	**Dómine,**	**cálicem**	**salutáris,**	**tuam**
We offer	to You,	Lord,	the chalice	of salvation,	your

	n	a			ab	
deprecántes	**cleméntiam:**	**ut**	**in**	**conspéctu**	**divínae**
asking	mercy	that	in	the sight	of divine

	g	g		ab		g	g
majestátis	**tuae,**	**pro**	**nostra**	**et**	**totíus**	**mundi**
majesty	Your	for	our	and	of all	the world

	ab		ab		g		s
salúte,	**cum**	**odóre**	**suavitátis**	**ascéndat.**	**Amen**
salvation,	with	an odor	of sweetness	it may ascend.

	ab		g			ab	ab
In	**spíritu**	**humilitátis**	**et**	**in**	**ánimo**	**contríto**
In	a spirit	of humility	and	in	a soul	contrite

	s			ab	v	
suscipiámur	**a**	**te,**	**Dómine,**	**et**	**sic**
may we be received	by	You,	Lord,	and	so

	s		n	n		ab	ab
fiat	**sacrifícium**	**nostrum**	**in**	**conspéctu**	**tuo**
may be made	sacrifice	our	in	sight	Your

	s		d	v	v
hódie	**ut pláceat**	**tibi,**	**Dómine**	**Deus.**
today	that it may please	You,	Lord	God.

---

humilitas, -tatis, f.: *humility (from* **humus,** *ground, earth)*

animus, animi, m.: *animate*

contritus: *contrite (from* **contero, -tere, -trivi, -tritus,** *to break down, to crush)*

placeo, placere, placui, placatus: *please, placid, pleasure*

sanctificator, -toris, m.: *sanctify, sanctification*

benedico, -dicere, -dixi, -dictus: *benediction*

praeparo, -parare, -paravi, -paratus: *prepare*

calix, calicis, m.: *calyx, chalice*

deprecor, deprecari, deprecatus: *deprecate*

clementia, clementiae, f.: *clement, inclement*

conspectus, conspectus, m.: *conspicuous*

totus, -a, -um (Gen. totius): *total*

odor, odoris, m.: *odor*

suavitas, suavitatis, f.: *suave*

As you go on, notice in the same way the compounds of **fero, ferre, tuli, latus**—to carry, bear: in such obvious forms as **offero,** and less obvious ones like **oblatio,** and the English derivatives— relate, prelate, inference, suffer, etc.*

capio, capere, cepi, captus, to take—(**suscipiamur, accipiens**) receive, perceive, conceive, deceive, etc.

specio, specere, spexi, spectus, to look (**conspectus, respicere, despicio**) species, respect, prospect, perspective.

We have of course only given a few examples of each. You will find more in the Latin, and many more English derivatives in your own vocabulary. Here are the main prepositions used in making compounds. You have met most of them already. If you look them up in the vocabulary at the end of the book, you will see how often they are used in compounds.

These prefixes cannot be used alone

a, ab: away
ad: to, towards
ante: before
circum: around
com, con (cum): together, or forcibly
de: down
in: in, on, against
inter: between, to pieces
ob: towards
sub: under, up from under
super: upon, over and above
per: through, thoroughly

amb: around, about
dis, di: asunder, apart
pro: forward
red: re—again
sed: se—apart
in: not

The word, **dies,** day, has various useful compounds:

diurnus—daily; **biduum,** space of two days; **triduum,** space of three days.
meridiem—middle of the day, noon; **ante-meridiem** (A.M. morning); **post meridiem** (P.M. afternoon).
hodie—**hoc die,** on this day—today.
pridie—**pro-die,** the day before.
cottidie—daily (**quotidie**), "panem nostrum **quotidianus** da nobis hodie."
postridie—**postero die,** the day after.

---

* See page 190.

67

imp.	v	v	v	v		
Veni,	**sanctificátor,**	**omnípotens**	**aetérne**	**Deus,**	**et**	
Come,	sanctifier,	almighty	eternal	God,	and	

imp.	a	a	d	d	d
bénedic	**hoc**	**sacrifícium,**	**tuo**	**sancto**	**nómini**
bless	this	sacrifice,	for Your	holy	Name

a
praeparátum.
prepared.

i		a	a	a	
Lavábo	**inter**	**innocéntes**	**manus**	**meas,**	**et**
I will wash	among	the innocent	hands	my,	and

i	a	a	v		s
circumdábo	**altáre**	**tuum,**	**Dómine,**	**ut**	**aúdiam**
will give around	altar	Your,	Lord,	that	I may hear

a	g	s	a	a	
vocem	**laudis,**	**et**	**enárrem**	**univérsa**	**mirabília**
the voice	of praise,	and	may tell	all	wonderful things

a	v	i	a	g	g
tua.	**Dómine,**	**diléxi**	**decórem**	**domus**	**tuae**
Your.	Lord,	I have loved	the beauty	of house	Your

	a	g	g	g		s
et	**locum**	**habitatiónis**	**glóriae**	**tuae.**	**Ne**	**perdas**
and	the place	of the dwelling	of glory	Your.	Do not	destroy

	ab	v	a	a			ab
cum	**ímpiis,**	**Deus,**	**ánimam**	**meam,**	**et**	**cum**	**viris**
with	the impious,	God,	soul	my,	and	with	men

g	a	a
sánguinum	**vitam**	**meam.**
of blood(s)	life	my.

---

lavo, -are, -avi, lautus: *lave, lavatory*
vox, vocis, f.: *vocal, vocabulary, vocation*
enarro, -are, -avi, -atus: *narrate*
decus, decoris, m.: *decorous, decorate, decorum*
perdo, -ere, -didi, -ditus: *perdition*
sanguis, sanguinis, m.: *sanguine, sanguinary*

We will point out a few more things about this formation of words, and then leave it to your own interest and intelligence.

In the Liturgy, you will find a great many adjectives used as nouns. These when masculine or feminine, of course refer to people, as **impii,** on the opposite page, meaning 'impious ones'. Or **'Cum sanctis tuis in aeternum',** 'With Your holy ones forever' and so on. And when such an adjective is neuter, it refers to things— **mirabilia,** wonderful things. **Sancta sanctorum,** Holies of Holies. So don't expect a noun in Latin, just because we need one in English.

Besides adding prefixes in front of words, you can add suffixes at the end and change the kind of word, rather than the meaning. For instance, to form nouns showing the agent, or doer, of an action, **-tor (sor),** m., or **-trix,** f., are added to roots and verb-stems —**sanctificator,** from **sanctificatus, genitor, genitrix** from **genitus,** the past participle of **gignere.**

To make abstract nouns:

-ia: **innocentia** from **innocens**
-tas: **humilitas** from **humilis**
-tudo: **magnitudo** from **magnus**
-io: **habitatio** from **habitus**

Adjectives are formed with **-ulus, -olus,** to make diminuitives and these are used as nouns: **filiolus,** a little son, from **filius.**

Adjectives meaning full of, with **-osus, -lens, -lentus: gloriosus, periculosus.**

Adjectives meaning pertaining to, with **-alis, -aris, -elis, -ilis, -ulis: facilis,** from **facio, humilis** from **humus,** ground.

This is only a hint as to possible suffixes. You will absorb most of the main ones as you go along, but if you want a complete list, you will have to look in a large Latin grammar. If you look at the vocabulary at the end of the book, you will see many words together made from the same root, as **gloria, glorifico, gloriosus.**

	g	ab	n	i	n
In	quorum	mánibus	iniquitátes	sunt,	déxtera
In	whose	hands	iniquities	are,	the right hand

	g	i	ab	n	
eórum	repléta	est	munéribus.	Ego	autem	in
of them	filled	is	with gifts.	I	however	in

ab	ab	i	imp.	a	
innocéntia	mea	ingréssus sum:	rédime	me	et
innocence	my	have walked:	redeem	me	and

imp.	g	n	n	i	
miserére	mei.	Pes	meus	stetit	in
have mercy	on me.	Foot	my	has stood	in

ab		ab	i	a	v
dirécto:	in	ecclésiis	benedícam	te,	Dómine.
the direct way:	in	the assemblies	I will bless	You,	Lord.

	n	d	d	d	d		ab
Glória	Patri	et	Fílio	et	Spirítui	Sancto, sicut erat in princípio et

a g

nunc et semper, et in saécula saeculórum.   Amen

---

repleo, -plere, -plevi, -pletus: *replete, complete*
munus, muneris, n.: *remunerate, munificent*
ingredior, ingredi, ingressus: *progress, digress, aggression*
redimo, redimere, redemi, redemptus: *redeem*
pes, pedis, m.: *pedal, pedestrian, centipede*
directum, -i, n.: *direct*
ecclesia, -ae, f.: *ecclesiastic*

PRONOUNS

A pronoun (for, or instead of a noun) is a word which indicates some person or thing without naming or describing it. Some people think that the first words were pronouns, and that "I", "you" and so on, are developments of the original caveman's grunt as he pointed to himself, or to his wife!

Personal pronouns indicate a person or object in itself, without reference to where it is, or what it is. In Latin these are **ego, tu, nos** and **vos,** and if you don't know what these are in English by now, you can look at page 173, on which you will also find the other case-forms of each. In Latin there is no personal pronoun for he, she, it or they. You use a demonstrative pronoun instead, to make it quite clear which 'he' you are talking about. Personal pronouns are not used in the Nominative, as subjects of verbs, unless special emphasis is needed. On the opposite page the Psalmist wants to emphasize his own innocence, and so says: **"Ego, autem in innocentia mea ingressus sum."**

Possessive pronouns are usually used as adjectives, as in English, my foot, your wig. They are adjectives of the first and second declension: **meus, tuus, suus, noster, vester, suus.**

Demonstrative, or 'showing' pronouns, are used to point out a person or thing, and are also used as adjectives (that, or that chair). There are five different sets of these, enabling you to indicate what you are talking about much more precisely than in English.

Is, ea, id (that) is used in the most indefinite sort of pointing out, for any person or thing that is not the subject of the sentence. (For instance on the opposite page, you see **dextera eorum,** the right hands of them.) You have probably gathered that **is** is the masculine Nominative singular, **ea** the feminine, and **id** the neuter, but you will find the complete declension on page 173.

imp	v	v	a	a	a	d
Súscipe,	**sancta**	**Trínitas,**	**hanc**	**oblatiónem,**	**quam**	**tibi**
Receive,	holy	Trinity,	this	oblation,	which	to you

i		a	g		g
offérimus	**ob**	**memóriam**	**passiónis,**		**resurrectiónis**
we offer	for	the memory	of the Passion,		resurrection

g	g	g	g	g		
et	**ascensiónis**	**Jesu**	**Christi,**	**Dómini**	**nostri,**	**et**	**in**
and	ascension	of Jesus	Christ,	Lord	our,	and	in

a	g	g		g	
honórem	**beátae**	**Maríae**	**semper**	**Vírginis,**	**et**
honor	of blessed	Mary	ever	Virgin,	and

g	g	g		g	g
beáti	**Joánnis**	**Baptístae,**	**et**	**sanctórum**	**Apostolórum**
of blessed	John	the Baptist,	and	of the holy	Apostles

g		g		g		g	g
Petri	**et**	**Pauli,**	**et**	**istórum**	**et**	**ómnium**	**sanctórum,**
Peter	and	Paul,	and	of these	and	of all	the Saints,

	d	s		a	d		
ut	**illis**	**profíciat**	**ad**	**honórem,**	**nobis,**	**autem,**	**ad**
that	them	it may profit	to	honor,	us,	however,	to

a		n		abl	inf.		s
salútem:	**Et**	**illi**	**pro**	**nobis**	**intercédere**	**dignéntur**
salvation.	And	they	for	us	to intercede	may deign

	ab	g	a	i		ab
in	**caelis,**	**quorum**	**memóriam**	**ágimus**	**in**	**terris,**
in	heaven,	whose	memory	we celebrate	on	earth,

	a	a	a	a	
per	**eúndem**	**Christum**	**Dóminum**	**nostrum.**	**Amen**
through	the same	Christ	Lord	our.	

---

oblatio, -onis, f.: *oblation*
memoria, -ae, f.: *memory*
intercedo, -cedere, -cessi, -cessus: *intercede*
ago, agere, egi, actus: *act, active*

Hic, haec, hoc (this) point out a person or thing near the speaker. **Ille, illa, illud** (that) point out a person or thing far from the speaker. **Iste, ista, istud** (that) point out something somewhere in between.

On the opposite page you see examples of the last two: "Ut **illis** proficiat ad honorem ... et **illi** pro nobis intercedere dignentur ..." "**istorum** et omnium sanctorum ..."

Isdem, eadem, idem (the same) is just like **is, ea, id,** with the addition of an unchangeable suffix, **-dem.** "Per **eundem** Christum Dominum nostrum".

Ipse, ipsa, ipsum (self) is also called an intensive pronoun, and is used by itself or with a noun for emphasis, just as we do in English: "Jane did it **herself**". You see a striking example of it later in the Mass: '**per ipsum, et cum ipso, et in ipso**'. (Page 98.)

Relative Pronouns, **qui, quae, quod** (who, which) are those which bad writers of English always use too frequently. They relate, or connect a clause with a noun in the main sentence, as **which** does in the previous sentence. Sometimes in English we let the relative pronoun be understood and not expressed as in "The book you took yesterday was mine", but in Latin it is always stated clearly. There are two things to be noticed about a relative pronoun:

1. It may be in any case in its own clause. For instance in **"Quam** tibi offerimus", on the opposite page, **quam** is in the Accusative case, as the object of **offerimus** or in **"quorum** memoriam agimus", **quorum** is in the Genitive.

2. It refers back to a noun or pronoun in the main sentence, or a previous clause. This noun or pronoun is called the **antecedent,** or walker-before, of the relative pronoun, which must agree with it in gender and number, since both the antecedent and the relative pronoun are talking about the same thing. For instance, the antecedent of **quam** in the above example is **oblationem,** which is a feminine singular noun. So **quam** must also have a feminine singular form.

imp   v   n   n   n

Oráte, fratres, ut meum ac vestrum sacrifícium
Pray, brothers, that my and your sacrifice

n   s   a   a

acceptábile fiat apud Deum Patrem
acceptable may be made with God the Father

a   s   n   a

omnipoténtem. Suscípiat Dóminus sacrifícium de
almighty. May receive the Lord sacrifice from

ab   ab   a   a   g   g

mánibus tuis ad laudem et glóriam nóminis sui
hands your to the praise and glory of name His

a   a   g   g   g

ad utilitátem quoque nostram, totiúsque Ecclésiae suae
to profit also our, and of all Church His

g

sanctae. Amen
holy.

Secreta*

ab   ab   i   v   g

In méntibus nostris, quaésumus, Dómine, verae
In minds our, we ask, Lord, of the true

g   a   imp   n   a

fidéi sacraménta confírma: ut qui concéptum
faith the sacraments strengthen: that we who conceived

ab   a   a   a   i

de Vírgine, Deum verum ac hóminem confitémur,
of the Virgin, God true and man confess,

g   g   g   a

per ejus salutíferae resurrectiónis poténtiam,
through of His health-bringing resurrection the power,

a   inf   a   a

ad aetérnam mereámur perveníre laetítiam. Per eúndem
to eternal we may merit to arrive joy.

a   a

Dóminum nóstrum.

---

* Secreta comes from secerno, -ere, secrevi, secretus to set aside, separate
(the bread and wine to be consecrated).

The Interrogative Pronouns, **quis, quid** (who? what?) are, of course, used for asking questions, just as in English. The only point is to be careful you do not confuse them with the Relative pronouns, as several of the forms are the same. (See page 174.)

There are various other pronouns which are modifications of those already given, such as **aliquis,** someone; **quisquam,** anyone. See page 175.

The Reflexive, or bending-back pronoun, **se,** and its corresponding possessive adjective **suus,** which we listed under possessive pronouns, are only used in reference to the subject of the sentence, for instance, on the opposite page: "gloriam nominis **sui",** to the glory of His Name. **Sui** can only refer to the subject of the sentence, which is **Dominus.** In the same way "Ecclesiae **suae** sanctae", can only be the Church of the Lord, and not the somewhat undefined "His" of the English. If any other "he" was meant, the appropriate form of **is,** or **hic,** or **ille,** would be used, as in the Secret Prayer on the opposite page: "Per **ejus** salutiferae resurrectionis potentiam". **Ejus** does not refer to the subject of the sentence, which is the "we" in **mereamur,** so **sui,** "of Him," the reflexive pronoun, or **'suae',** His, possessive adjective, cannot be used.

You have now been given all the main kinds of pronouns. Look at their declensions on page 173, and be sure that you could recognize each of them in its various cases. Then go through the Latin of the Mass from the beginning of this book, find all the pronouns, and see if you know which kind each is, and what work it is doing in the sentence.

You may have noticed that there is more than one way of saying 'and' in Latin. **Et** is one word, but when you see **et . . . et,** it means 'both . . . and'.

Ac and **atque** are other ways of saying 'and'.

-que added on to a word also means 'and', as in **totiusque** on the opposite page.

Quoque (to which + and) means 'also'.

75

    a   a   g   n   ab

Per ómnia saécula saeculórum. Amen. Dóminus vobíscum. Et cum

 ab   ab   a

spíritu tuo. Sursum corda. Habémus   ad
                 Up   hearts. We have (them lifted up)   to

 acc   a   s   d   d   d

Dóminum. Grátias agámus Dómino   Deo nostro.
the Lord. Thanks let us give to the Lord God our.

 n   n   i

Dignum et justum est.
Worthy and just   it is.

        n   n   i   n   n

Vere dignum et justum est, aequum et salutáre,
Truly worthy and just   it is, right   and good,

 a   d   a   inf

nos tibi semper et ubíque grátias ágere,
for us to You always and everywhere thanks to give,

 v   v   v   v   v   v

Dómine sancte, Pater omnípotens, aetérne Deus: Et
Lord holy, Father almighty, eternal God: And

 a   ab   g   g   g

te in Veneratióne beátae Maríae semper Vírginis
You in the Veneration of blessed Mary always a Virgin

 inf   inf   inf   n

collaudáre, benedícere, et praedicáre. Quae et
to praise, bless,   and glorify.   Who also

 a   a   g   g   ab

Unigénitum tuum Sancti Spíritus obumbratióne
Only-Begotten Your of the Holy Spirit by the overshadowing

 i   g   ab   ab   a

concépit, et virginitátis glória permanénte, lumen
conceived, and of virginity the glory remaining, the Light

 a   d   i   a   a

aetérnum mundo effúdit, Jesum Christum,
eternal to the world shed forth, Jesus Christ,

 a   a

Dóminum nostrum.
Lord our.

Following the Preface for Feasts of Our Lady on the opposite and following pages, you will find the Prefaces of Masses for the Dead, and of Corpus Christi and Christmas. The Propers of these Masses are given later in the book, but their Prefaces are placed here because (a) This is the place where they come in the Missal, (b) They provide examples of various grammatical points which should be explained here and now.

VERBAL NOUNS

We have already considered verbs as verbs, and verbs used as adjectives, or participles. There are also verbs used as nouns. In English you can say, "I like to swim", "Swimming is fun", or "I like swimming" or "It is a good place for swimming", all of which sentences use the verb 'swim' as a noun.

Now in the case of "I like **to swim**" you are using the infinitive as a noun, the object of the verb 'like'. I like what? I like to swim. So in Latin, the infinitive can be the subject or object of the verb. "Justum est gratias agere." It is just to give thanks. Now when the sentence gets more complicated, as it actually is, "Justum est . . . nos tibi gratias agere", the infinitive is still being used as a noun, but it has a subject, **nos,** and an indirect object, **Tibi,** and is being used as a verb at the same time. When you are translating it into English, you have to say "It is right for us to give thanks", or ". . . that we should give thanks"; but we can also use the same construction as the Latin in such a sentence as "Mother wants me to buy her a pair of stockings", in which 'me' is the subject of the infinitive 'to buy'.

	a	a	a	i	n
Per	**quem**	**majestátem**	**tuam**	**laudant**	**Ángeli**
Through	Whom	majesty	Your	praise	the Angels,

	i	n	i	n	n
adórant	**Dominatiónes,**	**tremunt**	**Potestátes**	**caeli**
adore	the Dominions,	tremble	the Powers,	and Heavens

	g	n		n	n
caelorúmque	**Virtútes**	**ac**	**Beáta**	**Séraphim**
of the heavens	the Virtues	and	the blessed	Seraphim

	ab	ab	i		ab
sócia	**exsultatióne**	**concélebrant.**	**Cum**	**quibus**	**et**
with sociable	exultation	celebrate.	With	whom	also

	a	a		inf.		s
nostras	**voces**	**ut**	**admítti**	**júbeas**
our	voices	that	to be admitted	You may command

	i	ab	ab	
deprecámur,	**súpplici**	**confessióne**	**dicéntes . . .**
we ask,	suppliant	confession	saying . . .

	v	v	v	v	v	v
Sanctus,	**Sanctus,**	**Sanctus,**	**Dóminus**	**Deus**	**Sabáoth.**
Holy,	Holy,	Holy,	Lord	God	of Hosts.

	n	i	n		n	ab	ab
Pleni	**sunt**	**caeli**	**et**	**terra**	**glória**	**tua.**
Full	are	the heavens	and	the earth	with glory	Your.

	n	ab	n	n	
Hosánna	**in**	**excélsis.**	**Benedíctus**	**qui**	**venit**	**in**
Hosanna	in	the highest.	Blessed	He who	comes	in

	ab	g	n	ab
nómine	**Dómini.**	**Hosánna**	**in**	**excélsis**
the name	of the Lord.			

---

laudo, -are, -avi, -atus: *laudatory*
tremo, -ere, -ui: *tremor, tremble*
admitto, -ere, -misi, -missus: *admit*
deprecor, -ari, -atus: *deprecate*

Now you have probably observed that in English or Latin, the subject of an infinitive is not in the Nominative case, but in the Accusative. The reason for this is shown in the sentence: "Mother wants me to buy her a pair of stockings". At first both 'me' and 'to buy' were considered to be objects of the verb 'want', as on the opposite page, both **nostras voces** and **admitti** are the objects of the verb **jubeas.** 'Our voices' are commanded, and 'to be admitted' is commanded. But gradually in such cases the noun was considered to be the subject of the infinitive, and so the subject of any infinitive, wherever you find it, came to be in the Accusative case.

This is really all there is to that mysterious construction which Caesar used so often, called Oratio Obliqua, or Indirect Discourse. It is a way of saying what someone said or felt or commanded, without a direct quotation, by means of an infinitive used as the object of the verb of saying, or commanding, or feeling, with a subject of its own.

As you see we do the same thing in English, but Latin has a different choice of verbs after which an infinitive may be used in this way, and they are usually just the verbs which English would not use. But it is perfectly easy to see what is meant by the Latin. For instance here: ". . . that you may command our voices to be admitted", is perfectly good English. In Latin you could also say, "He *declared* our voices to be admitted", whereas for good English you would have to change it round to "He declared that our voices were admitted . . .".

	n		n		n		n
Vere	dignum	et	justum	est,	aequum	et	salutáre,
Truly	worthy	and	just	it is,	right	and	good,

	d				a	inf
nos	tibi	semper	et	ubíque	grátias	ágere,
us	to You	always	and	everywhere	thanks	to give,

v	v	v	v	v	v
Dómine	sancte,	Pater	omnípotens,	aetērne	Deus,
Lord	holy	Father	almighty,	eternal	God,

	a		a	a	ab	d
per	Christum	Dóminum	nostrum,	in	quo	nobis
through	Christ	Lord	our,	in	Whom	to us

n	g		g		i	
spes	beátae	resurrectiónis	effúlsit,	ut
the hope	of a blessed	resurrection	has shone forth,	that

a	i	n	g	n	a
quos	contrístat	certa	moriéndi	condício	eósdem
whom	saddens	the certain	of dying	condition,	the same

s	g	g	n	d
consolétur	futúrae	immortalitátis	promíssio.	Tuis
should console	of future	immortality	the promise.	For your,

	d	v	n	i	i
enim	fidélibus,	Dómine,	vita	mutátur,	non	tóllitur,
indeed,	faithful,	Lord,	life	is changed,	not	taken away,

	ab		g	g	g
et	dissolúta	terréstris	hujus	incolátus
and	having been dissolved	of earthly	this	sojourn

ab	n	ab	n	i
domo	aetérna	in caelis	habitátio	comparátur.
the house	an eternal	in heaven	home	is prepared.

Et ídeo cum Angelis . . .

---

effulgeo, -ere, -fulsi, fulsus: *effulgent*
muto, -are, -avi, -atus: *mutation*
tollo, -ere, sustuli, sublatus: *tolerant*

In both English and Latin you can use the infinitive as a noun when it is the subject or object of a verb. But you cannot use an infinitive as an indirect object. You cannot say: 'This is a good place for to swim,' you have to say: 'This is a good place for swimming.' So in Latin there is another verbal noun called the Gerund, to correspond to our form of the verb 'swimming'. You see an example on the opposite page: certa **moriendi** condicio, 'the certain condition of dying.'

You can always recognize a gerund when you see one, by the **nd,** which occurs both in its name, and in every actual gerund before its case-ending, as in morie**ndi.** There is no nominative case, since the infinitive is used for that purpose, but there is a genitive, ending **ndi,** a dative, **ndo,** an accusative for use after prepositions, **ndum,** and an ablative, **ndo.** An idea of something to be done is contained in the English verbal noun "A good place for swimming"; this is also true of the Latin gerund, whence its name, from the verb **gero, gerere, gessi, gestus,** 'to do'. This is its 'gerund' form and means something to be done or something doing.

There is a corresponding verbal adjective, or participle called the Gerundive, which you will hear more about when we come to an example.

And there is one other sort of verbal noun, which is very rarely used, called the Supine. It is a fourth declension noun, is only used in the Accusative and Ablative Cases, and looks like the past passive participle, except for the fourth declension ending **u.** The Accusative form is used to express purpose after verbs of notion, the Ablative in such expressions as **Mirabile dictui:** (wonderful to relate). You are not likely to need one, so there is no need to explain it further. The only reason for mentioning it at all is that it gives grammarians a convenient name for the last principal stem of verbs. Intransitive verbs can have no perfect passive participle, but they could have a Supine, if anyone wanted to use it, so the stem from which the Perfect Passive Participle (if any), the Future Infinitive, etc. are derived, is usually called the Supine stem, to include all kinds of verbs. (See pages 52–53, and footnote, page 197.)

Vere	dignum	et	justum	est,	aequum	et	salutáre,
Truly	worthy	and	just	it is,	right	and	good,

nos	tibi	semper	et	ubíque		grátias	ágere,
us	to You	always	and	everywhere		thanks	to give,

Dómine	sancte,	Pater	omnípotens,	aetérne	Deus:	Quia,
Lord	holy,	Father	almighty,	eternal	God:	For,

per	incarnáti		Verbi	mystérium	nova	mentis
through	of the incarnate		Word	the mystery	new	of mind

nostrae	óculis	lux	tuae	claritátis	infúlsit:
our	to the eyes	light	of Your	brightness	has shone,

ut,	dum	visibíliter	Deum	cognóscimus,	per	hunc
that,	while	visibly	God	we recognize,	through	Him

in	invisibílium	amórem	rapiámur.
into	of things invisible	the love	we may be carried.

Et	ídeo,	cum	Ángelis	et	Archángelis,	cum
And	therefore	with	Angels	and	Archangels,	with

Thrónis	et	Dominatiónibus,	cúmque	ómni	milítia
Thrones	and	Dominations	and with	all	the army

caeléstis	exércitus,	hýmnum	glóriae	túae
of the heavenly	host,	the hymn	of glory	your

cánimus,	síne	fíne	dicéntes,	Sanctus,	Sanctus,
we sing,	without	end	saying	Holy,	Holy,

Sanctus.
Holy.

By this time, you should have learned how to 'guess' at the meaning of a new Latin word—that is, how to use your knowledge of English in order to know more Latin.

Also you know how to find out the case of a noun and the mood of a verb. A good plan would be to mark the rest of the Latin for yourself.

You now have all the tools necessary for understanding Church Latin. That is, you know the forms and the uses of prepositions, nouns, pronouns, adjectives, verbs, adverbs, verbal adjectives and verbal nouns. All you need is practice in using them, and some clues about disentangling the more complicated kinds of sentences.

If you are not fairly sure of all the different forms—declensions and conjugations, now is the time to do something about it. If you have followed the suggestions as given, when you see a noun, adjective or pronoun, you should be able to tell its declension and case, and the reason for the case, and when you see a verb to tell its person, tense and mood. You should have practised this sufficiently on the pages where a translation is given, to be able to do so where the translation is not given, not for the sake of mental gymnastics, but for the sake of finding out the sense.

If you are more than a little hazy at this point, and continue without clearing your difficulties, Latin will be a slightly more intelligible blur, but still a blur.

———————

Grammatically speaking, there are three different kinds of sentences, simple, compound and complex. A simple sentence has only one verb. "The boy hit the ball". A compound sentence has two or more verbs independent of each other, but joined together by a conjunction (a joining-together, **con-iungo**) like **'and'**, or **'but'**. "The boy hit the ball and it broke the window." A complex sentence has one main verb, and one or more clauses, each with its own verb, which are braided (complex—**complecto, plecto,** to braid) into one whole. **"Because he broke the window,** he was fined ten cents." A clause from the Latin **clausa,** 'shut off', or 'enclosed', is probably so called because it is a unit shut off, or 'enclosed' from the rest of the sentence, with a subject, verb and so on.

Te	ígitur,	clementíssime	Pater,	per	Jesum
You	therefore,	most kind	Father,	through	Jesus

Christum,	Fílium	tuum,	Dóminum	nostrum,	súpplices
Christ,	Son	Your,	Lord	our,	entreating

rogámus	ac	pétimus,	uti	accépta	hábeas		et
we ask	and	seek,	that	accepted	You may have		and

benedícas	haec	dona,	haec	múnera,	haec	sancta
bless	these	gifts,	these	presents,	these	holy

sacrifícia	illibáta,	in	primis		quae	tibi
sacrifices	unimpaired,	in	the first place		which	to you

offérimus	pro	Ecclésia	tua	sancta	cathólica,	quam
we offer	for	Church	Your	holy	Catholic,	which

pacificáre,		custodíre,		adunáre	et	régere
to make peaceful,		to guard,		unite	and	rule

dignéris	toto	orbe	terrárum,	una	cum
You may deign	in all	the orb	of the lands,	together	with

fámulo tuo	Papa	nostro	*N.	et	Antístite	nostro
servant Your	Pope	our	N.	and	Bishop	our

N.	et	ómnibus	orthodóxis	atque	cathólicae		et
N.	and	all	orthodox	and	of the catholic		and

apostólicae	fidéi	cultóribus.
apostolic	faith	worshippers.

---

* 'N', of course, is an abbreviation for 'Nomen', name. The Pope's name now being Pius, the whole phrase is **una cum Papa nostro Pio,** as the preposition **cum** takes the Ablative Case. See if you can put your Bishop's name in the Ablative Case too, to fill in the 'N' after **Antistite nostro.**

Dependent clauses can only be used in three ways, as nouns, as adjectives, or as adverbs. Here is a sentence with one of each: "When Mary was walking down the street, it unfortunately happened that she slipped on a yellow banana peel which was lying on the sidewalk." 'Happened' is the main verb. What happened? 'She slipped on a banana peel'. So 'that she slipped . . .' is equivalent to a noun, the subject of 'happened'. '. . . which was lying on the sidewalk' describes the banana peel, in the same way as does 'yellow', so this clause is equivalent to an adjective. 'When Mary was walking down the street' tells us the time, and therefore modifies, or describes the verb in the same way as does 'unfortunately', so that this clause is equivalent to an adverb.

CLAUSES USED AS ADJECTIVES

Adjectival clauses are 'woven into' the sentence by Relative Pronouns or Relative Adjectives (see page 73) as in the example on the previous page. " . . . **which** was lying on the sidewalk . . ." **Which** is a relative pronoun, whose antecedent is **banana peel.** So on the opposite page, **quae tibi offerimus** is a relative or adjectival clause, introduced by the relative pronoun **quae,** whose antecedent is **sacrificia.** And **quam pacificare digneris** is another relative clause, introduced by **quam,** whose antecedent is **Ecclesia.** In the clause **quae tibi offerimus,** the verb is in the indicative mood, because the clause simply tells a fact about **sacrificia.** But in **quam pacificare digneris,** the verb is in the subjunctive mood because the clause contains the idea of a wish, a prayer.

Meménto, Dómine, famulórum   famularúmque
Be mindful, Lord,   of (men) servants   and of (women) servants

tuárum,   *N. et N.   et   ómnium   circumstántium   quorum
Your   and   all   those standing around   whose

tibi   fides   cógnita   est   et   nota   devótio,   pro
to you   faith   known   is   and   known   devotion,   for

quibus   tibi   offérimus   vel   qui   tibi   offérunt   hoc
whom   to You   we offer   or   who   to You   offer   this

sacrifícium   laudis,   pro   se   suísque   ómnibus
sacrifice   of praise,   for   themselves   and all   their (things)

pro   redemptióne   animárum   suárum,   pro   spe   salútis
for   redemption   of souls   their,   for   hope   of salvation

et   incolumitátis   suae   tibíque   reddunt   vota   sua
and   safety   their   and to You   pay   vows   their,

aetérno   Deo,   vivo   et   vero.
eternal   God,   living   and   true.

---

* If you would like to pray for your friends, in Latin, put their names into the proper cases—here, the Genitive. You can find the Latin version of a Saint's name in a Missal or Breviary, and sometimes it is not what you would expect. For instance, for some strange reason, the Latin for "Guy" is Vitus! If you are ever in a Public Library with a little spare time, look in the Catholic Directory at the Latin names of the American Dioceses. They are given in the Genitive, Archdiocese of New York: Archidioecesis Neo-Eboracensis.

Here are three more relative clauses. You see that the antecedent of each of the relative pronouns, **quorum, quibus** and **qui,** is 'famulorum famularumque et omnium circumstantium.' The verbs in the clauses are all in the indicative, because the clauses are simply telling facts about the antecedents.

CLAUSES USED AS NOUNS

A noun clause may be the Subject of the sentence. **"That you have wronged me** doth appear in this." In Latin the accusative and infinitive construction is often used in this way where English would use a clause. "Dignum est **gratias agere."** "It is meet **to give thanks,"** or "that we should give thanks."

A noun clause may also be used in apposition with a noun, that is, placed in the same position as a noun already in the sentence. On the opposite page the names you put in for **N. et N.** are in apposition with **famulórum famularúmque.** So in the sentence "The fact **that you have wronged me** doth appear in this," the clause is in apposition with the noun **fact.** "Ipse enim spiritus testimonium reddit spiritui nostro, **quod sum filii Dei."** "The Spirit Himself gives testimony to our spirit **that we are sons of God."** The clause is in apposition with the noun **testimonium.**

All this may seem fairly obvious, but when you are making your own translation of Latin, you will find that you need to know all the possibilities about noun clauses.

Communicántes et memóriam venerántes in primis
Communicating and memory venerating in the first place

gloriósae semper Vírginis Maríae Genetrícis Dei
of the glorious always Virgin Mary Mother of God

et Dómini nostri, Jesu Christi, sed et beatórum
and Lord our, Jesus Christ, also too of blessed

Apostolórum ac Mártyrum tuórum, Petri et Pauli, Andréae, Jacóbi,

Joánnis, Thomae, Jacóbi, Philíppi, Bartholomaéi, Matthaéi, Si-

mónis et Thaddaéi, Lini, Cleti, Cleméntis, Xysti, Cornélii, Cypriáni,

Lauréntii, Chrysógoni, Joánnis et Pauli, Cosmae et Damiáni, et

ómnium Sanctórum tuórum, quórum méritis precibúsque
of all Saints Your, whose to merits and prayers

concédas, ut in ómnibus protectiónis tuae
grant, that in all things of protection Your

muniámur auxílio. Per eúndem Christum
We may be fortified by the help. Through the same Christ

Dóminum nostrum. Amen
Lord our.

Hanc ígitur, oblatiónem servitútis nostrae, sed et
This, therefore, oblation of service our, and also

cunctae famíliae tuae, quaésumus, Dómine, ut placátus
of all family Your, we ask, Lord, that pleased

accípias: diésque nostros in tua pace dispónas,
you may accept: and days our in Your peace You may dispose,

atque ab aetérna damnatióne nos éripi
and from eternal damnation us to be snatched

et in electórum tuórum júbeas grege
and in of chosen your You may order in the flock

numerári, Per Christum Dóminum nostrum. Amen.
to be numbered.

A noun clause may also be the Object of the Verb. "I know **that you have wronged me.** The clause is the object of the verb **know.** Noun clauses, as well as the infinitive and accusative construction are most frequently found as objects of verbs meaning 'to feel', 'to know', 'to grant', 'to ask'. If the clause simply states a fact, its verb is in the indicative mood. "Scientes **quia Dominus est."** "Knowing that it is the Lord." But if the clause includes the idea of purpose, or wish, or hope, the verb is in the subjunctive, as on the opposite page. "Concedas **ut . . . muniamur."** "Quaesumus **ut accipias atque jubeas . . ."**

Various conjunctions may introduce noun clauses, but the one you will meet most frequently in the Mass is **ut,** as above. The negative form is **ut non.** "Praesta **ut** in me **non** remaneat scelerum macula." "Grant that the stains of sin may not remain in me." For other conjunctions introducing noun clauses, see page 117.

CLAUSES USED AS ADVERBS

Adverbial clauses do the same work as adverbs, giving you such information as the time, place, reason for the main action of the sentence. The only thing to learn about them is the meaning of the different conjunctions which introduce them into sentences.

Final Clauses, which tell you the purpose of the action, are introduced by that useful word **ut.** "Hic venit **ut testimonium perhiberet de lumine."** "He came that He might bear witness to the light." The negative form of **ut** when it introduces a final clause is **ne.** "Libera eas de ore leonis **ne absorbeat eas tartarus."** "Free them from the mouth of the lion lest Hell should swallow them."

Result or Consequence Clauses are introduced by **ut,** or **ita ut.** "Sic enim dilexit Deus mundum **ut Filium suum unigenitum daret."** "God so loved the world that He gave His only Son."

Quam **oblatiónem** **tu,** **Deus,** **in ómnibus,** **quaésumus,**
Which oblation You, God, in all things, we ask,

benedíctam, **adscríptam,** **ratam,** **ratíonábilem**
blessed, consecrated, approved, reasonable

acceptabilémque **fácere** **dignéris,** **ut** **nobis**
and acceptable to make You may deign, that for us

Corpus **et** **Sanguis** **fiat** **dilectíssimi**
the Body and Blood may be made of most beloved

Fílii **tui,** **Dómini** **nostri,** **Jesu** **Christi,** **Qui**
Son Your, Lord our, Jesus Christ, Who

prídie **quam** **paterétur,** **accépit** **panem**
the day before that He suffered, took bread

in **sanctas** **ac** **venerábiles** **manus** **suas,** **et**
into holy and venerable hands His, and

elevátis **óculis** **in** **caelum,** **ad** **te,**
having been lifted eyes into heaven, to You,

Deum **Patrem** **suum** **omnipoténtem,** **tibi** **grátias**
God Father His all-powerful, to You thanks

agens, **benedíxit,** **fregit,** **dedítque** **discípulis** **suis,**
giving, blessed, broke, and gave to disciples His,

dicens: **Accípite** **et** **manducáte** **ex** **hoc** **omnes,**
saying: Take and eat of This all (you),

Hoc **est** **enim** **Corpus** **meum.**
This is indeed Body My.

from /

de ab

sanudo. unique. gente

dolore homine

ante — before

apud — by, near, among

circa — about around / concerning

secundum: according to   Circum around

supra: a upon above / upon   Contra: against

a ab abs: from by   inter: among between

Cum- together with   justa: near

de: from down to / concerning   praeter: except, besides, beyond

e, ex: out of / within   per: through, by means of

                              propter: on account of, because of

                              post: after behind

pro: for, on behalf of   cg (acc)   at a (abl)

prae- before. because of   in (acc)   ef e (abl)

sine: without   de (abl)

sub: under, below

in: with ablative: in or at

super with ablative: concerning

about

                              in with accusative: onto

super with accusative: over on top of about,

                              beyond

of — to

in — into

acc. Montem grandem

to tell you where you

how where you

acc — casting of those object of

of those object of the thing

tabernacle

Confiteor...

... Introibo ad altare Dei. Ad deum
qui laetificat juventutem meam
... Confitebor tibi in cithara. Deus
Deus meus quare tristis es Anima mea
et quare conturbas me? Spera in Deo
quoniam adhuc confitebor illi. —
Salutare vultus mei et Deus meus
Gloria Patri et Filio et Spiritui Sancto.
sicut erat in principio et nunc et semper
et in saecula saeculorum ... Amen

TIME WHEN

In English when we want to indicate the time or circumstances connected with the main thought of a sentence, we usually use an adverbial-clause beginning 'While ...' or 'When'. In Latin they also have another way all their own. You see an example of this on the opposite page: **Elevatis oculis,** which is translated literally as "Eyes having been lifted". You see that **oculis** is in the Ablative case, and as **elevatis** is a participle, it agrees with its noun and is in the Ablative case also. This construction in not a clause—it contains no main verb, and there is no word which connects it with the main sentence. For this reason it is called the Ablative Absolute construction. 'Absolute' because it is ab-solved, or loosed (from the verb **solvo,** to loose, as in 'absolution') from the main sentence. The noun and participle are in the Ablative as that is the case for indicating time or attendant circumstances anyway. In classical Latin, they used a noun and a participle (usually the perfect), in this way, or two nouns, or a noun and an adjective. In Ecclesiastical Latin a noun with a present participle is more frequent than in classical Latin. Later in the Mass you will come across, **Intercedente beata et gloriosa Virgine Maria,** "the blessed and glorious Virgin Mary interceding. ...."

You see the difference between this construction and something like **Tibi gratias agens** on the opposite page. The participle **agens** here is in the Nominative, agreeing with the subject of the sentence **qui,** as does **dicens.** But **elevatis** is in the Ablative, agreeing with **oculis** and is quite separate from the main sentence.

Símili	modo	postquam	cenátum*	est,	accípiens
In the same	way	after	dined	it was,	taking

et	hunc	praeclárum	Cálicem	in sanctas	ac	venerábiles
also	this	splendid	Chalice	in holy	and	venerable

manus	suas:	item	tibi	grátias	agens,	benedíxit,
hands	His:	again	to You	thanks	giving,	He blessed

dedítque	discípulis	suis,	dicens:	Accípite	et	bíbite
and gave	to disciples	His,	saying:	Take	and	drink

ex	eo	omnes,	Hic	est	enim	Calix	Sánguinis
of	this	all you,	This	is,	for,	the Chalice	of Blood

mei,	novi	et	aetérni	testaménti,	mystérium
My,	of the new	and	eternal	testament,	the mystery

fídei,	qui	pro	vobis	et	pro	multis	effundétur
of faith,	which	for	you	and	for	many	shall be shed

in	remissiónem	peccatórum.	Haec	quotiescúmque
into	remission	of sins.	These things	as often as

fecéritis,	in	mei	memóriam	faciétis.
you shall do,	in	of Me	the memory	you shall do.

---

* **Ceno, cenare** means 'to dine', **cena** is a dinner. 'Cenaculum' is a dining-room. So the Cenacle Congregation took its name from the dining-room in which the Last Supper was celebrated, and in which Our Lady and the Apostles waited and prayed for the coming of the Holy Ghost.

In addition to the Ablative Absolute way of expressing Time or Attendant Circumstances, you can use an ordinary adverbial clause, as in English. There are two on the opposite page. Such clauses are introduced by:

cum, ut, quando:	when	**dum:**	while, until
antequam, priusquam:	before	**donec, quando:**	until
postquam:	after		

Clauses of **PLACE WHERE** are introduced by: **ubi, quo:** where, whither, **unde:** whence.

Clauses of **CAUSE**, giving the reason for the action, by: **quia, quoniam, quod, eo quod, cum,** meaning 'since', 'because', 'for'. (See p. 119)

Clauses of **CONCESSION** by **cum, quamvis, etsi, licet,** meaning 'although'.

Clauses of **CONDITION** by **si,** if, **nisi,** unless

Clauses of **COMPARISON** by **ut, sicut, sicuti, prout, quomodo, tamquam, quasi**—as, as if

All the kinds of clauses there are have now been given. In the rest of the Mass, you will meet mostly Relative clauses, Noun clauses and Final or Purpose clauses.

Cenatum est, "It was dined" is what is called an Impersonal verb because it doesn't tell you who did it. The participle **cenatum** agrees with a neuter subject, 'it', understood. We use such verbs in talking about the weather, "it is fine", "it rained". In Latin they use it for such statements, and for "It was a pity", "It is right", etc. just as we would. They also use it for such things as 'It grieves me', **miseret me;** 'it shames me', **pudet me.** And of course, 'it happens', **accidit;** 'it is necessary', **necesse est;** 'it is permitted', **licet.** But in Latin the use of such verbs is extended to the passive of an intransitive verb, like 'dine' or 'fight'. They say "It was dined", or "it was fought". In English, we are always told to avoid impersonal constructions if possible, and to use 'It', or 'one' with great care and rarity. But this is not so in Latin, the best writers used this impersonal construction frequently.

Unde et **mémores, Dómine, nos servi** **tui** **sed**
Whence also mindful, Lord, we servants Your, and

et **plebs** tua **sancta, ejúsdem** **Christi** **Fílii** tui,
also people Your holy, of the same Christ Son Your,

Dómini nostri, tam beátae **passiónis** nec **non et** ab
Lord our, so of blessed passion and also from

ínferis **resurrectiónis, sed** et **in** caelos **gloriósae**
lower places of resurrection and also in heaven of glorious

ascensiónis, **offérimus** **praeclárae** **majestáti** tuae de
ascension, we offer to splendid majesty Your from

tuis **donis** ac **datis,** **hóstiam** **puram, hóstiam**
your gifts and presents a victim pure, victim

sanctam, **hóstiam** **immaculátam, Panem** **sanctum vitae**
holy, victim unstained, the bread holy of life

aetérnae, et **Cálicem** **salútis** **perpétuae.**
eternal, and the Chalice of salvation perpetual.

Supra **quae** **propítio** ac **seréno** **vultu respícere**
On which propitiously and with serene face to look

dignéris: et **accépta** **habére,** **sícuti accépta**
may you deign and accepted to consider, as accepted

hábere, **dignátus es** **múnera** **púeri** **tui** **justi**
to consider You deigned the gifts of servant Your just,

Abel et **sacrifícium** **Patriárchae** nostri **Ábrahae,** et
Abel and the sacrifice of Patriarch our Abraham, and

quod **tibi** **óbtulit** **sumus** **sacérdos** **tuus Melchísedech,**
what to You offered high priest Your Melchisedech

sanctum **sacrifícium,** **immaculátam** **hóstiam.**
holy sacrifice, unspotted victim.

We have been talking about main verbs in sentences, clauses dependent on them and so on, and it now seems necessary to find out what a sentence really is. In theory it should be a "set of words complete in itself, containing subject and predicate and conveying a complete statement, question or command". It is the unit of written or spoken language. In writing, we end a sentence with a period, because that is equivalent to the longest voice-pause. When you are writing you can go back and see whether each sentence contains a set of words complete in itself. You do not need to connect sentences by 'ands' and 'buts' and 'whiches' because the eye carries over, and can go back and check up. But the Liturgy was designed in speech and to be spoken, not to be read. It was written down and the punctuation put in long afterwards. Therefore, what sounds well, not what looks well, regulates the sentences and pauses.* For instance, as printed, there is a full-stop after **perpetuae,** on the opposite page, but the thought and the grammatical sentence goes right on with a relative clause, **Supra quae** . . . and the antecedents of **quae** are **hostiam, panem, calicem** in the previous sentence. You should not do that in good English writing, but you would do it in speaking, where you naturally use longer sentences and connect them up more fully. So do not let the punctuation of the Liturgy worry you. The rules of English punctuation only apply in their original use of longer or shorter pauses. You will not necessarily find a complete sentence, on either side of a colon, or a period. If you cannot find a main verb where you expect it, let common sense guide you and look further.

----

* All the same, we have somewhat simplified the punctuation of the Latin as given in the Missal, occasionally substituting commas for colons or periods.

95

Súpplices **te** **rogámus,** **omnípotens** **Deus,** **jube**
Suppliants You we ask, almighty God, command

haec **perférri** **per** **manus** **sancti** **Ángeli** **tui** **in**
these to be carried by hands of holy Angel Your on

sublíme altare **tuum,** **in** **conspéctu** **divínae** **majestátis**
sublime altar Your, in sight of divine majesty

tuae, **ut** **quotquot** **ex** **hac** **altáris** **participatióne**
Your, that as many from this of the altar participation

sacrosánctum **Fílii** **tui** **Corpus** **et** **Sánguinem**
the most holy of Son Your Body and Blood

sumpsérimus, **omni** **benedictióne** **caelésti** **et** **grátia**
we shall receive, with all blessing heavenly and with grace

repleámur, **per** **eúndem** **Christum** **Dominum**
shall be filled through the same Christ Lord

nostrum. **Amen.**
our.

Meménto **étiam,** **Dómine,** **famulórum famularúmque** **tuárum**
Be mindful also, Lord of servants Your,

N. et. N., **qui** **nos** **praecessérunt** **cum** **signo**
N. and N. who us have gone before with the sign

fídei, **et** **dórmiunt** **in** **somno** **pacis.** **Ipsis,**
of faith, and sleep in the sleep of peace. To them,

Dómine, **et** **ómnibus** **in** **Christo** **quiescéntibus** **locum**
Lord and to all in Christ resting a place

refrigérii, **lucis** **et** **pacis** **ut** **indúlgeas,**
of refreshment, light and peace That you may grant,

deprecámur. **Per eúndem Christum Dóminum nostrum.** **Amen.**
we ask.

You should be worried by the fact that **famulorum,** etc. are obviously in the Genitive Case and yet are the objects of the verb **memento.** The verb **memini,** to remember, be mindful of, is an odd word anyhow. It has only perfect tenses, no present or future, and these are used as if they were the corresponding tenses in the present or future. The perfect does the work of the present, the pluperfect of the perfect and so on.

Also **memini,** and its opposite, **obliviscor,** to forget, take the Genitive Case when they mean 'to be forgetful of', or 'mindful of', just as we use the preposition 'of' after them in English. When they mean literally to retain in the mind, or to forget completely, they take the Accusative.

Misereor, to pity, or have pity, also may take the Genitive (**Miserere mei**) and sometimes the Dative, (**miserere nobis,** 'Have mercy on us'.) The English equivalent usually shows you why these and various other verbs behave this way. In such cases, the noun is not really the direct object of the action. If you are mindful, or pitiful, the object of the action is really your own mind.

In the same way, there are five deponent verbs* which are followed by the Ablative Case, and it is easy to see why they should be when you look at their meaning.

Utor, I employ myself (with)   **vescor,** I feed (on)
fruor, I enjoy (myself with)   **potior,** I have power (over)
fungor, I busy myself (with)

In all five, the English sense demands a preposition, which would be followed by the Ablative if we had cases in English.

---

* See page 57.

Nobis   **quoque**   **peccatóribus,**   **fámulis**   **tuis**   **de**
To us   also,   sinners,   servants   Your,   from

multitúdine   **miseratiónum**   **tuárum**   **sperántibus,**   **partem**
the multitude   of mercies   Your   hoping,   part

áliquam   **et**   **societátem**   **donáre**   **dignéris**   **cum**   **tuis**
some   and   company   to give   deign,   with   Your

sanctis   **Apóstolis et Martýribus: cum Joánne, Stéphano, Matthía,**
holy

Bárnaba, Ignátio, Alexándro, Marcellíno, Petro, Felicitáte, Per-

pétua, Agatha, Lúcia, Agnéte, Caecília, Anastásia, et   ómnibus
                                         and   all

Sanctis   **tuis,**   **intra**   **quórum**   **nos**   **consórtium,**   **non**
saints   Your,   among   whose   us   company,   not

aestimátor **mériti,**   **sed véniae,**   **quáesumus,**   **largítor**
estimator   of merit, but   of pardon,   we ask,   (as) the granter

admítte,   **Per Christum Dóminum nostrum, per**   **quem**
to admit.   through   Whom

haec   **ómnia,**   **Dómine,**   **semper**   **bona**   **creas,**
these   all,   Lord,   always   good things   You create

sanctíficas,   **vivíficas,**   **benedícis**   **et**   **praestas**   **nobis.**
sanctify,   vivify,   bless   and   give   to us.

Per   **ipsum,**   **et**   **cum**   **ipso,**   **et**   **in**   **ipso,**   **est**
Through   Him,   and   with   Him,   and   in   Him,   is

tibi   **Deo**   **Patri**   **omnipoténti,**   **in**   **unitáte**
to you   God   the Father   all mighty,   in   the unity

Spíritus   **Sancti,**   **omnis**   **honor**   **et**   **glória.**   **Per ómnia**
of the Spirit   Holy,   all   honor   and   glory.

sáecula saeculórum.   **Amen.**

In the rest of the text of the Mass, we shall point out each clause, telling you which kind of a clause it is and the reason for the mood of its verb. As you are reading the Latin, consider the clauses in this way as you come to them, and then refer to the explanation to see if you were right. The object of such exercises is to make each clause contribute its full quota to the meaning of the sentence. A certain amount of it is necessary because the Latin order of clauses is often quite different from the usual English order. Do not try to fit them around into a good English sentence, but find out what they mean where they stand in the Latin text.

But a knowledge of grammar and syntax is only one means toward the end of learning Church Latin as a mother-tongue. The other and more important means is actually to use Latin. A certain amount of theory is necessary in order to learn anything intelligently, but a large amount of practice is even more essential. You can read a book on Golf in Ten Lessons, but your game will not improve until you get out on the course and practise what you have learned. So while you are making yourself more and more familiar with Latin grammar and syntax as amplified and reviewed in the following pages, try to learn at least one Latin prayer a week. First, of course, comes the Pater Noster (page 100) and the Ave Maria (page 149). The Confiteor, Gloria and Credo, the Salve Regina (page 149), the Litany of Loretto (page 150), the prayers in the Offertory of the Mass and before Communion are the next obvious choices. When you are using these prayers as confidently in Latin as in English, you have all your favorite prayers and hymns to learn in their original language. Latin hymns, in particular, are easy to learn by heart and wonderful to recite when walking or driving or strap-hanging. Say them aloud whenever possible, to accustom your ears to the sound and rhythm of Latin. This is much more valuable than merely familiarizing your eyes with Latin words in black and white. Prayers are meant to be said, not read.

Orémus: Praecéptis   salutáribus móniti et   divína
Let us pray: By precepts healthful   taught, and by divine

institutióne formáti,   audémus dícere: Pater noster qui
institution strengthened, we dare to say: Father our   who

es in caelis, sanctificétur   nomen tuum, advéniat
are in heaven, be sanctified may name Your, come may

regnum   tuum: fiat   volúntas tua,   sicut in
kingdom Your. Be done may Will   Your, as   in

caelo et in terra: panem nostrum cotidiánum da
heaven so on earth: bread our   daily   give

nobis hódie, Et   dimítte nobis débita nostra sicut
to us today, And forgive us   debts our,   as

et   nos dimíttimus debitóribus nostris, Et   ne   nos
also we   forgive   debtors   our   And not us

indúcas in   tentatiónem, sed líbera nos a   malo.
lead   into temptation, but free us from evil.

Amen.

Here is a chance to compare the use of the Imperative and the Subjunctive moods. You see that the first three things we ask in the Our Father are all put into the Subjunctive. Father McNabb says that these are what we should be working for and hoping for, but which we cannot do anything to bring about by our unaided efforts. We have no right to say to God "Make Your Kingdom come". So it is put into the subjunctive to be more realistic.

There are various grammatical names for the different shades of meaning of the subjunctive used in independent clauses, but common sense will tell you whether it is expressing an exhortation, command, a concession, a hope and so on.

But **da** and **dimitte** are both in the imperative, and **ne inducas** is a negative command, because, as Father McNabb says, we have a right to these, if we are working and hoping for the fulfillment of the first three things.

There are various ways of telling somebody not to do something in Latin. In poetry, they use the imperative with **non** before it. Another way is to say **Noli**, or **nolite** (plural)* with the infinitive of the verb,—"Do not wish to do it". Another way is the one used here, **ne**, or **non**, with either the present or perfect subjunctive. And still another way is to use **Vide** and then **ne** and the present or perfect subjunctive "See that you do not...."

Líbera nos, quaésumus, Dómine, ab ómnibus malis,
Free us, we ask, Lord, from all evils,

praetéritis, praeséntibus et futúris. Et, intercedénte
past, present and future. and, interceding

beáta et gloriósa semper Vírgine Dei Genitríce
blessed and glorious always Virgin of God the mother

María, cum beátis Apóstolis tuis Petro et Paulo,
Mary, with blessed Apostles Your Peter and Paul,

atque Andréa et ómnibus Sanctis, da
and Andrew and all the Saints, give

propítius pacem in diébus nostris: ut, ope
propitiously peace in days our, so that, by the work

misericórdiae tuae adjúti, et a peccáto simus
of mercy Your helped, both from sin we may be

semper líberi et ab omni perturbatióne secúri,
always free, and from all disquiet secure,

per eúndem Dóminum nostrum Jesum Christum, Fílium tuum

qui tecum vivit et regnat, in unitáte Spíritus Sancti, Deus per

ómnia saécula saeculórum. Amen.

Pax Dómini sit semper vobíscum. Et cum spíritu tuo.

Haec commíxtio et consecrátio Córporis et
May this commingling and consecration of the Body and

Sánguinis Dómini nostri Jesu Christi fiat
Blood of Lord our Jesus Christ be made

accipiéntibus nobis in vitam aetérnam. Amen.
to receiving us into life eternal.

Agnus Dei, Qui tollis peccáta mundi,
Lamb of God, Who takes away the sins of the world,

miserére nobis.
have mercy on us.

Agnus Dei, Qui tollis peccáta mundi, miserére nobis.

Agnus Dei, Qui tollis peccáta mundi, dona nobis pacem.

Quaesumus, Domine is just thrown in. **Libera ... et ... da ... ut ... simus** shows the main progress of the sentence.

Intercedente Virgine Maria is an Ablative Absolute, with a present participle.

Adjuti is a participle, agreeing with the subject of **simus** (contained in the verb), we, the congregation at Mass.

Ut simus liberi et securi. Simus is in the subjunctive because it is a clause showing purpose.

Qui vivit et regnat ... is a simple relative clause.

Sit and **fiat** are both 'jussive' or 'commanding' subjunctives.

Qui tollis peccata mundi is a relative clause.

Dómine	Jesu	Christe,	qui	dixísti	Apostólis	tuis:
Lord	Jesus	Christ,	Who	said	to Apostles	Your:

Pacem	relínquo	vobis,	pacem	meam	do	vobis:
Peace	I leave	to you,	peace	my	I give	to you:

ne	respícias	peccáta	mea,	sed	fidem	Ecclésiae
do not	look at	sins	my,	but	at the faith	of Church

tuae:	eámque	secúndum	voluntátem	tuam	pacificáre
Your,	and her	according to	Will	Your	to make peaceful

et	coadunáre	dignéris:	Qui vivis et regnas, Deus per ómnia
and	to unite	deign:	

saécula saeculórum. Amen.

Dómine	Jesu	Christe,	Fili	Dei	vivi,	qui	ex
Lord	Jesus	Christ,	Son	of God	living,	Who	from

voluntáte	Patris,	cooperánte	Spíritu	Sancto,
the will	of the Father,	working together	the Spirit	Holy,

per	mortem	tuam	mundum	vivificásti:	líbera	me
through	death	Your	the world	made living:	free	me

per	hoc	sacrosánctum	Corpus	et	Sánguinem	tuum
through	this	most holy	Body	and	Blood	Your

ab	ómnibus	iniquitátibus	meis,	et	univérsis	malis:
from	all	iniquities	my,	and	from all	evils:

et	fac	me	tuis	semper	inhaerére	mandátis,
and	make	me	to your	always	cling	to commandments,

et	a	te	numquam	separári	permíttas:
and	from	You	never	to be separated	allow:

Qui cum eódem Deo Patre et Spíritu Sancto vivis et regnas Deus

in saécula saeculórum. Amen.

Ne respicias . . . digneris are the key words.

Qui dixisti is a relative clause, describing **Domine Jesu Christe.**

Pacem relinquo vobis, pacem meam do vobis, are direct quotations, and so need no grammatical connections.

Ne respicias, is a negative command.

Digneris is a 'jussive' subjunctive.

Qui vivis is a relative clause, referring back to **Domine Jesu Christe.**

The next prayer is put together in the same way.

Qui vivificasti is a relative clause, attached to **Domine Jesu Christe.**

Cooperante Spiritu Sancto is ablative absolute, using a present participle.

Libera and **fac** are straight commands, as **numquam permittas** is a negative one. The negative contained in **numquam** takes the place of the **ne** you have met before.

Separari is an infinitive used as a noun, the object of **permittas**

And **qui vivis** again refers back to **Domine Jesu Christe.**

Percéptio   Córporis   tui,   Dómine   Jesu   Christe,
The reception of Body   Your,   Lord   Jesus   Christ,

quod   ego   indígnus   súmere   praesúmo,   non   mihi
which   I   unworthy   to take   presume,   not   to me

provéniat   in   judícium   et   condemnatiónem: sed   pro
may result   in   judgment   and   condemnation,   but   by

tua   pietáte   prosit   mihi   ad   tutaméntum   mentis
Your   kindness   may it avail   me   to   protection   of mind

et   córporis,   et   ad   medélam   percipiéndam.   Qui vivis
and   body,   and   to   a remedy   to be received.

et regnas cum Deo Patre in unitáte Spíritus sancti Deus, per

ómnia saécula saeculórum.   Amen.

Panem   caeléstem   accípiam   et   nomen   Dómini
Bread   heavenly   I shall take   and   the name   of the Lord

invocábo.
I will call on.

Dómine,   non   sum   dignus   ut   intres   sub
Lord,   not   I am   worthy   that   you should enter   under

tectum   meum: sed   tantum   dic   verbo,   Et
roof   my,   but   only   speak   with a word,   And

sanábitur   ánima   mea.
shall be healed   soul   my.

        Corpus   Dómini   nostri   Jesu   Christi   custódiat
(May) The Body   of Lord   our   Jesus   Christ   keep

ánimam   meam   in   vitam   aetérnam.   Amen.
soul   my   into   life   eternal.   Amen.

Quod ego indignus sumere presumo is a relative clause, describing Corporis.

Non proveniat is in the subjunctive expressing a wish, as is **prosit.**

Percipiendam is an example of a **gerundive** (see page 81). As you see, it is a form of the verb used as an adjective, giving the idea of purpose, or necessity, or duty, of something **to be done.** Gerundives are first and second declension adjectives and have the **nd** which the gerund also has, coming before the case-endings.

Ut intres, is subjunctive in a clause of result.

Custodiat is a subjunctive of wishing.

Quid **retríbuam** **Dómino** **pro** **ómnibus** **quae**
What shall I return to the Lord for everything which

retríbuit **mihi?** **Cálicem** **salutáris** **accípiam**
He has given me? The Chalice of salvation I shall take,

et **nomen** **Dómini** **invocábo.** **Laudans**
and the name of the Lord I shall call on. Praising

invocábo **Dóminum,** **et** **ab** **inimícis** **meis** **salvus**
I shall call on the Lord and from enemies my safe

ero.
I shall be.

     Sanguis **Dómini** **nostri** **Jesu** **Christi** **custódiat**
(May) The Blood of Lord our Jesus Christ keep

ánimam **meam** **in** **vitam** **aetérnam.** **Amen.**
soul my into life eternal. Amen.

Quod **ore** **súmpsimus,** **Dómine,** **pura** **mente**
What by mouth we have taken, Lord, in a pure mind

capiámus: **et** **de** **múnere** **temporáli** **fiat**
may we receive and from a gift temporal may it be

nobis **remédium** **sempitérnum.**
for us a remedy eternal.

Corpus **tuum,** **Dómine,** **quod** **sumpsi,** **et**
(May) Body Your, Lord, which I have taken, and

Sanguis **quem** **potávi** **adhaéreat** **viscéribus** **meis,**
Blood which I have drunk, cling to bowels my,

Et **praesta** **ut** **in** **me** **non** **remáneat** **scélerum**
And grant that in me not may remain of sins

mácula, **quem** **pura** **et** **sancta** **refecérunt**
the stains, whom pure and holy have re-made

sacraménta. **Qui vívis et regnas in saécula saeculórum.** **Amen.**
sacraments.

Quid shows you that a question is coming, an interrogative pronoun, like the English **what**.

Quae retribuit mihi is a relative clause, used as an adjective describing **omnibus**.

Custodiat is a subjunctive of wishing.

Quod ore sumpserimus is a clause used as a noun, the object of **capiamus**.

and **capiamus** and **fiat** are again subjunctives because they express a wish.

Quod sumpsi and **quem potavi** are relative clauses used as adjectives describing **Corpus** and **Sanguis**.

Ut . . . non remaneat is a clause of purpose, with the verb in the subjunctive.

Quem refecerunt sacramenta is a relative clause, describing **me.**

Communio

Ecce,	Vírgo	concípiet	et	páriet	Fílium:	et
Behold,	a Virgin	shall conceive	and	bear	a Son:	and

vocábitur	nomen	ejus	Emmánuel.
shall be called	name	His	Emmanual.

Postcommunio

Grátiam	tuam,	quaésumus,	Dómine,	méntibus	nostris
Grace	Your,	we ask,	Lord	into minds	our

infúnde:	ut,	qui,	Angelo	nuntiánte,	Christi,	Fílii
pour:	that,	who,	an Angel	announcing,	of Christ,	Son

tui,	incarnatiónem	cognóvimus:	per	passiónem	ejus
Your,	the incarnation	we know:	through	passion	His

et	crucem,	ad	resurrectiónis	glóriam
and	Cross,	to	of the resurrection	the glory

perducámur.	Per eúndem Dóminum.
we may be lead through.	

Concipiet, pariet and **vocabitur** are simple indicative future.

Angelo nuntiante is an Ablative Absolute;

Qui . . . cognovimus is a relative clause, describing the subject understood of **perducamur.**

Ut . . . perducamur is a purpose clause. The verb is in the subjunctive.

Dóminus	vobíscum.		Et cum	spíritu	tuo.	Ite,
The Lord	be with you.		And with	spirit	your.	Go,

missa	est.	Deo	grátias.
the sending	is.	To God	thanks.

Pláceat	tibi,	sancta	Trínitas,	obséquium	servitútis
May please	you,	holy	Trinity,	the homage	of service

meae:	et	praesta	ut	sacrifícium	quod	óculis
my,	and	grant	that	the sacrifice	which	in the eyes

tuae	majestátis	indígnus	óbtuli,	tibi	sit
of Your	majesty	unworthy	I offered,	to you	may be

acceptábile;	mihíque	et	ómnibus	pro	quibus	illud
acceptable;	and to me	and	to all	for	whom	it

óbtuli,	sit,	te	miseránte,	propitiábile,	Per Christum
I offered,	be,	You	having mercy,	propitious,	

Dóminum nostrum.	Amen.

Benedícat	vos	omnípotens	Deus,	Pater,	et	Fílius,
Bless	you	almighty	God,	Father,	and	Son

et Spíritus	Sanctus.	Amen.
and Spirit	Holy.	

Missa is the feminine form of the past participle used as a noun.

Placeat is again a jussive subjunctive.

Ut sacrificium sit acceptabile is a clause of purpose.

Quod . . . obtuli is a relative clause, used as an adjective, describing sacrificium.

Sit acceptabile et sit propitiabile are jussive subjunctives.

Pro quibus illud obtuli is a relative clause, describing omnibus.

Benedicat is jussive subjunctive.

Dóminus vobíscum. Et cum spiritu tuo.

Inítium   sancti   Evangélii   secúndum   Joánnem.
The beginning of the holy Gospel   according to John.

Glória   tibi,   Dómine.
Glory   to You,   Lord.

In princípio   erat Verbum,   et   Verbum   erat apud
In the beginning was the Word,   and   the Word   was with

Deum,   et   Deus   erat   Verbum.   Hoc   erat   in
God,   and   God   was   the Word.   This   was   in

princípio   apud   Deum.   Ómnia   per   ipsum
the beginning with   God.   All things through   Him

facta   sunt,   et   sine   ipso   factum   est   nihil
made   were,   and   without Him   made   was   nothing

quod   factum   est.   In   ipso   vita   erat,   et   vita   erat
which   made   was.   In   Him   life   was,   and   life   was

lux   hóminum,   et   lux   in   ténebris   lucet,
the light of men,   and   the light   in   darknesses   shines,

et   ténebrae   eam   non   comprehendérunt.
and   the darknesses   it   not   did engulf.

Fuit   homo   missus a   Deo,   cui   nomen erat
There was a man   sent   from   God,   whose   name   was

Joánnes. Hic   venit in testimónium, ut   testimónium
John.   This man   came for a testimony, that   witness

perhibéret   de   lúmine,   ut   omnes   créderent
he might give   of   the light, that   all   might believe

per   illum.   Non   erat   ille   lux,   sed   ut
through Him.   Not   was   he   the light, but   that

testimónium perhibéret   de   lúmine. Erat   lux
witness   he might give of the   light. He was the light

vera   quae   illúminat omnem   hóminem veniéntem in
true   which   illumines every   man   coming   into

hunc   mundum.   In   mundo   erat   et   mundus
this   world.   In   the world he was,   and   the world

per   ipsum   factus   est,   et   mundus   eum   non
through Him   made   was,   and   the world Him   not

cognóvit. In   própria   venit,   et   sui
knew.   Into   His own possessions He came, and His own people

112

eum   non   recepérunt.   Quotquot,   autem,   recepérunt
Him   not   received.   Whoever,   however,   received,

eum   dedit   eis   potestátem   fílios   Dei   fíeri,
Him,   He gave   to them   power   sons   of God   to become,

his   qui   credunt   in   nómine   ejus,   qui   non   ex
To them   who   believe   in   name   His,   who   not   from

sanguínibus,   neque   ex   voluntáte   carnis,   neque   ex
blood,   nor   from   the will   of the flesh,   nor   from

voluntáte   viri,   sed   ex   Deo   nati   sunt.   Et   Verbum
the will   of man,   but   from   God   born   are.   And   the Word

caro   factum   est,   et   habitávit   in   nobis,   et   vídimus
flesh   made   was,   and   lived   among   us,   and   we saw

glóriam   ejus,   glóriam   quasi   Unigeníti   a   Patre,
glory   His,   glory   as   of the Only-Begotten   of the Father,

plenum   grátiae   et   veritátis.   Deo   grátias.
full   of grace   and   of truth.   To God   thanks.

Introitus

Dóminus dixit ad me: Fílius meus es tu, ego
The Lord said to me: Son my are You. I

hódie génui te. Quare fremuérunt gentes
today have begotten You. Why have raged the nations

et pópuli meditáti sunt inánia? Glória Patri.
and the peoples thought vain things.

Oratio

Deus, qui hanc sacratíssimam noctem veri
God, Who this most holy night of the true

lúminis fecísti illustratióne claréscere, da,
Light has made by the shining to grow bright, grant,

quaésumus, ut cujus lucis mystéria in terra
we ask, that of Whose light the mysteries on earth

cognóvimus, ejus quoque gaúdiis in caelo
we have known, His also joys in heaven

perfruámur. Qui tecum vivit et regnat in unitáte Spíritus
we may enjoy.

Sancti, Deus per ómnia saécula saeculórum. Amen.

Léctio Epístolae beáti Pauli Apóstoli ad Titum

Caríssime: Appáruit grátia Dei Salvatóris nostri
Dearly beloved: Has appeared the grace of God Savior our

ómnibus homínibus, erúdiens nos, ut, abnegántes
to all men, teaching us, that, denying

impietátem et saeculária desidéria, sóbrie et juste
impiety and worldly desires, soberly and justly

et pie vivámus in
and lovingly we may live in

QUESTIONS

Questions may be introduced by obviously interrogative words, such as **Quare,** why, on the opposite page: **cur,** also meaning why, **ubi,** where, **unde,** whence, or the interrogative pronoun, **quis, quid.**

If there is no such word, Latin does not usually trust to word-order and inflexion of voice as we do, but puts in a word to make it clear that the sentence is a question and not a statement.

If the expected answer to the question might be 'yes', or 'no', **-ne** is added to the emphatic word and this word is placed first in the sentence.

If the expected answer is 'yes', **nonne (non + ne)** is put in. **Nonne est hic faber?** Isn't He a carpenter?

If the expected answer is 'no', you find **non, num,** or **numquid. Numquid tu maior est patre nostro Jacob?** You aren't greater than our father Jacob, are you?

Double questions, (whether . . . or) have **-ne** or **utrum** (whether) in the first part, and **an,** (or), **anne,** (or) **necne** (nor) in the second. Sometimes **utrum** is left out, if the sense is clear without it. **"Quid est facilius dicere paralytico: dimmittuntur peccata: an dicere: Surge . . ."** What is easier to say to a paralytic: your sins are forgiven: or to say: arise . . .

Indirect Questions, that is, questions which do not quote the actual words of the speaker, are noun clauses. **Nescio ubi sim,** I don't know where I am. The verb in the clause is in the subjunctive because it does not express a statement of fact.

There is no one Latin word for 'yes' or 'no'. They use such expressions as: **vere,** truly; **etiam,** even so; **ita,** so; **certe,** certainly. And for 'no', **nullo modo,** by no means; or **minime,** not at all.

115

hoc   saéculo,   exspectántes   beátam   spem   et
this   world,   looking out for the blessed   hope   and

advéntum   glóriae   magni   Dei   et   Salvatóris
coming   of the glory of the great   God   and   Saviour

nostri Jesu   Christi,   qui   dedit   semetípsum   pro   nobis:
our   Jesus   Christ,   Who   gave   His very self   for   us:

ut   nos   redímeret   ab   omni   inquitáte,   et
that   us   He might buy back   from   all   injustice,   and

mundáret   sibi   pópulum   acceptábilem,   sectatórem
cleanse   for himself   a people   acceptable,   doers

bonórum   óperum.   Haec   loquére   et   exhortáre: In
of good   works.   These things speak   and   urge: In

Christo   Jesu,   Dómino   nostro.
Christ   Jesus,   Lord   our.

Graduale:

Tecum   princípium   in   die   virtútis   tuae:
With You   the beginning   in   the day   of strength   Your:

in   splendóribus   Sanctórum   ex   útero   ante
among   the splendors   of the Saints from   the womb   before

lucíferum   génui   te.   Dixit   Dóminus   Dómino
the morning-star have I begotten You.   Said   the Lord   to Lord

meo: Sede   a   déxtris   meis: donec   ponam   inimícos
my: Sit   at   right hand   my: until   I place   enemies

tuos   scabéllum   pedum   tuórum.   Allelúia, Allelúia. Dóminus
your   as footstool of feet   your.

dixit ad me: Fílius meus es tu. Ego hódie génui te. Allelúia.

Sequéntia Sancti Evangélii secúndum Lucam.

In   illo   témpore: Éxiit   edíctum   a   Caésare
At   that   time: Went out   an edict   from   Caesar

Augústo   ut   describerétur   univérsus   orbis.
Augustus   that   should be enrolled   the whole   world.

116

The English word with which a careful writer has most trouble is probably 'that'. 'That' may be:

1. A demonstrative Pronoun or Adjective, in which case the Latin equivalent is **ille**. "Give me that book", "Da mihi **illum** librum".

2. A Relative pronoun (in Latin **qui**). **Qui dedit semetipsum pro nobis.** Who gave Himself for us.

3. A conjunction expressing purpose, (in Latin **ut . . .**), as on the opposite page, . . . **ut redimeret,** . . .'that He might redeem us'.

4. A conjunction introducing a clause of consequence, (in Latin **ut,** or **ita ut**) as on the next page. This construction is rendered in Latin either by the Accusative and Infinitive construction. **"Fac me tecum flere"**, "make me to cry with you": or by **ut** and the subjunctive, as on the opposite page, "Exiit edictum . . . ut describeretur . . ." or by a clause introduced by **quod,** (that, because), **quia,** (that, for, because), **quoniam,** (for, since, that).

As you see, **ut** is a Latin word, which does almost as many things as the English **that.** When it is introducing a clause of purpose, or consequence, or a noun clause, and the verb in the clause is in the subjunctive, it is equivalent to 'that', or 'so that'. When the verb in the clause is in the indicative mood, **ut** may mean **as, when** or **where.**

5. A conjunction introducing a noun clause. 'Remember that I am here'.

117

Haec **descríptio** **prima** **facta** **est** **a** **praéside**
This enrollment first made was by the governor

Sýriae **Cyríno:** **et** **ibant** **omnes** **ut**
of Syria, Cyrinus, and was going all that

profiteréntur **sínguli** **in** **suam** **civitátem.** **Ascéndit**
they might be enrolled each in his own city. Went up

autem **et** **Joseph** **a** **Galilaéa** **de** **civitáte**
therefore also Joseph from Galilee from the town

Názareth, **in** **Judaéam** **in** **civitátem** **David,** **quae**
Nazareth, into Judea into the city of David, which

vocátur **Béthlehem:** **eo quod** **esset** **de** **domo** **et**
is called Bethlehem: because he was of the house and

família **David,** **ut** **profiterétur** **cum** **María,**
family of David, that he might be enrolled with Mary,

desponsáta **sibi** **uxóre** **praegnánte.** **Factum est**
espoused to him wife pregnant, It happened,

autem, **cum** **essent** **ibi,** **impléti** **sunt** **dies**
however, when they were there, completed were the days

ut **páreret.** **Et** **péperit** **fílium**
that she should bring forth. And she brought forth Son

suum **primogénitum** **et** **pannis** **eum** **invólvit,**
her first-born and in swaddling clothes Him wrapped,

et **reclinávit** **eum** **in** **praesépio,** **quia** **non** **erat**
and laid Him in a manger, for not was

eis **locus** **in** **diversório.**
for them place in the inn.

118

Quod also has many of the troubles of the English 'that'. It may be:

The Neuter Singular of the relative pronoun, as on the next page, "Gaudium magnum, **quod** erit omni populo".

A conjunction introducing a clause of cause, as on the opposite page: "**eo quod** esset de domo et familia David". (The **eo,** the ablative case of **id,** is an ablative showing cause, 'because of this, that'.

A conjunction introducing a noun clause, equivalent to 'that' as in "Recordare, Jesu pie, **quod** sum causa tuae viae".

This last use of **quod** is exclusively the property of Ecclesiastical Latin. The early translators of the Bible from Greek into Latin found that there were two Greek constructions similar to our "He said that the car was to be washed" and "He told us to wash the car". The second construction (the infinitive-and-accusative) already existed in Latin. For the first they began to use clauses introduced by **quod.** To make it more interesting, the Greek word meaning 'that', also meant 'because', or 'for', and there were two other conjunctions already existing in Latin meaning 'because' and 'for', so these also began to be used to mean 'that'.

These two conjunctions are: **Quia** and **quoniam.** They may have their original meaning of 'because', 'for', or they may be equivalent to 'that'. For instance, in Achaz' prophecy, (page 38), "Numquid parum vobis est molestos esse hominibus **quia** molesti estis et Deo meo" **quia** simply means 'that'. On the opposite page, "quia non erat eis locum in diversorio," **quia** means 'for', 'because'.

Sometimes, in the New Testament especially, you meet **quod, quia** or **quoniam** introducing the direct words of a speaker. **Et confessus est: quia non sum ego Christus:** And he confessed, "I am not the Christ".

Et	pastóres	erant	in	regióne	eadem	vigilántes,	et
And	shepherds	were	in	region	the same	watching,	and

custodiéntes	vigílias		noctis	super	gregem	súum.
guarding	the watches		of night	over	flock	their.

Et	ecce,	Ángelus	Dómini	stetit	juxta	illos,
And	behold,	the Angel	of the Lord	stood	by	them,

et	cláritas	Dei	circumfúlsit	illos,	et
and	the brightness	of God	shone around	them,	and

timuérunt	timóre	magno.	Et	dixit	illis
they feared	with a fear	great.	And	said	to them

Ángelus:	Nolíte	timére:	ecce	enim,	evangelízo
the Angel:	Do not	fear,	behold	for	I tell

vobis	gaúdium	magnum,	quod	erit	omni	pópulo:
to you	joy	great,	which	be shall	to all	people.

quia	natus	est	vobis	hódie	Salvátor,	qui	est
for	born	is	to you	today	a Saviour,	Who	is

Christus	Dóminus,	in	civitáte	David.	Et	hoc	vobis
Christ	the Lord,	in	the city	of David.	And	this	to you

signum:	Inveniétis	infántem	pannis		involútum
a sign:	You will find	the child	in swaddling-clothes		wrapped

et	pósitum	in	praesépio.	Et	súbito	facta	est
and	placed	in	a manger.	And	suddenly	made	was

cum	Ángelo	multitúdo	milítiae	caeléstis,	laudántium
with	the Angel	a multitude	of the army	heavenly,	praising

Deum	et	dicéntium:	Glória	in	altíssimis	Deo,	et
God	and	saying:	Glory	in	the highest	to God	and

in	terra	pax	homínibus	bonae	voluntátis.
on	earth	peace	to men	of good	will.

Cum is one more word which needs watching. It may be a preposition meaning 'with', or 'together with', as **cum Angelo**.

Or it may be a conjunction meaning 'when', as on the previous page, "Factum est autem **cum** essent ibi."

And **cum** may be a conjunction meaning 'since', or 'although'.

To be clear about all these words, you only need to know what the possibilities are. The context will tell you the rest.

SEQUENCE OF TENSES

If you are ever worried by the tense of a verb in a clause, of an infinitive, or of a participle, as compared with the tense of the main verb, remember that the time of any subordinate verbs in a sentence may be looked at from the point of view of the main action, as it was happening, or as it is being narrated. For instance in: "I said, 'I am here' ", you use the present tense in the quotation, because that was what you said. But if you make it an indirect quotation, it would be "I said that I was here", to make the subordinate verb in time agreement with the main verb. But with infinitives and participles, we use tenses showing how the action was related to the action of the main verb as it happened. "I want to laugh", "I wanted to laugh", both use the present tense of the infinitive. "Going down town I stubbed my toe", "Going down town I stub my toe", both use the present participle, because in both cases the action went on at the same time as the action of the main verb. So if the subordinate Latin tense does not make sense, see which point of view is used in the English equivalent, and whether the other one is being used in Latin.

———————

Offertórium. Laeténtur caeli et exsúltet terra
Be glad the heavens and rejoice the earth

ante fáciem Dómini: quóniam venit.
before the face of the Lord: for He comes.

Secreta: Accépta tibi sit, Dómine, quaésumus,
Acceptable to you be, Lord, we ask,

hodiérnae festivitátis oblátio: ut, tua grátia
of today's festivity the offering, that, Your grace

largiénte, per haec sacrosáncta commércia in
giving freely, through these most holy transactions, in

íllius inveniámur forma, in quo tecum est
His we may be found form, in Whom, with You, is

nostra substántia: Qui técum vivit et regnat in unitáte Spíritus
our substance.

Sancti, Deus per ómnia saécula saeculórum. Amen.

Communio. In splendóribus Sanctórum ex útero
In the splendors of the Holies, from the womb

ante lucíferum génui te.
before the day-star I begot You.

Post-Commúnio. Da nobis, quaésumus, Dómine Deus
Give us, we ask, Lord God

noster, ut, qui Nativitátem Dómini nostri Jesu
our, that, we who the Birth of Lord our Jesus

Christi mystériis nos frequentáre gaudémus, dignis
Christ in mysteries us to celebrate rejoice, by worthy

conversatiónibus ad ejus mereámur perveníre
conversations to of Him we may merit to arrive at

consórtium, Qui tecum vivit et regnat in unitáte Spíritus Sancti,
the company,

Deus per ómnia saécula saéculorum. Amen.

As you go through the Liturgy, it is pleasant to notice how many lovely words Latin has for light and gladness. The Collect for the Vigil of the Feast of Pentecost has almost all of them together.

"Praesta, quaesumus, omnipotens Deus: ut claritatis tuae super nos splendor effulgeat; et lux tuae lucis corda eorum, qui per gratiam tuam renati sunt, Sancti Spiritus illustratione confirmet", Here are **claritas, splendor, lux, illustratio, effulgere.** Notice the different flavors and overtones of each of them, which the English derivatives have lost to a large extent.

And for being glad, you have **laetare,** and **gaudere. (Gaudere** is a more demonstrative active sort of rejoicing.) And **exsultare,** which comes from **ex-sultare,** which means to keep jumping. So to exult is to jump (out) with joy.

Saltare is what is called an 'iterative' or 'intensive' verb. It adds **to** to the stem of the original verb which was **salire,** to jump, and with this **to** acquires the idea of repetition. Sometimes the meaning seems to change, but you can see what happened. So **iacere** means to throw, and **iactare** means to hurl, **dormire,** to sleep, **dormitare,** to be sleepy. You see they become first conjugation verbs when they become 'iterative'.

Another kind of verb to look for is an 'inceptive' or 'inchoative', which merely means 'to begin to do' something. In these you find **sco** added to the present stem. For instance, **clarescere,** to grow bright. From this sort of verb, we get our words like 'adolescent', someone beginning to become an adult, 'senescent', beginning to grow old.

SUMMARY

You have now been introduced to all the various parts of speech, their Latin forms and uses, and the ways of putting them together in sentences. You have all the tools necessary in order to increase your knowledge of Latin so that in time you can read the Liturgy, or Medieval Latin poetry, or the Fathers of the Church, or the Pope's encyclicals in their original language.

In the remaining pages of this book, you will find the Propers of two more Masses, with a literal translation underneath, as before. Go through these, and see if you know why each sentence means what it does. Then read over each sentence, as we said at the beginning of the book, and make it give its meaning to you directly from the Latin.

Then take each word separately, and see if you can give its syntax, that is, if you can explain why it has the form it has: if it is a noun, its declension and its case and the reason for it. If it is a verb: the person, tense and mood, and the reason for the mood. If you find that any particular kind of words give you trouble, review the forms and explanation of the forms of that kind of word. Then read the section as a whole over again, and see how much more clearly the meaning will shine out.

Then take the Latin with no translation. Do not try to translate it: try to find out what it means. If you do not recognize a word, look it up first in the vocabulary at the end of the book and only refer to the translation, which is given separately, if you really need it to find out how the words are put together.

If you have an English-and-Latin Missal, you can continue this process indefinitely. Try reading the Latin by itself, and only refer to the English when you must. But after awhile, remove all temptation to lapse into English by acquiring a plain Latin Missal. You can buy small convenient ones which are published for missionaries who cannot carry big heavy books about the country. You can also buy Latin Missals which are about the same size as English-Latin ones, but which weigh less and have much larger type. You will find yourself understanding much more Latin than you would expect, when you have to get the meaning from it or go without.

You can also practise your Latin on the rest of the Liturgy. If you are one of those people who say Prime for morning prayers, and Compline in the evening, you can find some of the pamphlets containing these two Hours which give both the English and Latin. But in time, you will find it much more satisfactory to own a real

124

Breviary. They are fairly expensive in this country, but less expensive than the English translation.

If you are a student of Philosophy, you also save money by knowing Latin. The works of St. Thomas, for instance, can be obtained in English, but they can be obtained much more cheaply in Latin.

If you want more Latin with an English translation, "The Hymns of the Breviary and Missal" by Rev. Matthew Britt, O. S. B., gives you both. It provides a literal English translation of each hymn, as well as one or more 'literary' ones.

For relaxation and Latin at the same time, there is a pleasant book called "Medieval Latin Lyrics", by Helen Waddell. You are given the Latin with a translation on the opposite page, which is not in the least literal. Many of the poems, in either language, are very beautiful, and others are very funny.

The more you practise reading Latin, the better you will understand it, so do not stop at the Latin of the Mass. Follow your Missal in Latin as an indispensable minimum, but do as much more as your time and strength permit.

Introítus

Cibávit	eos	ex	ádipe	fruménti,	allelúia:	et
He fed	them	from	fatness	of wheat,	alleluia,	and

de	petra	melle	saturávit	eos,	allelúia,
from	the rock	with honey	he filled	them,	

allelúia allelúia.	Exsultáte	Deo,	adjutóri	nostro:	jubiláte
	Exult	in God,	help	our,	rejoice

Deo	Jacob.	Glória Patri.
to the God	of Jacob.	

*Orátio

Deus	qui	nobis	sub	Sacraménto	mirábili
God	who	to us	in	Sacrament	wonderful

passiónis	tuae	memóriam	reliquísti:	tríbue,	quaésumus,
of passion	your	a memorial	has left	grant,	we ask,

ita	nos	Córporis	et	Sánguinis	tui	sacra	mystéria
so	us	of Body	and	Blood	your	the holy	mysteries

venerári,	ut	redemptiónis	tuae	fructum	in	nobis
to venerate,	that	of redemption	your	the fruit	in	us

júgiter	sentiámus:	Qui vivis et regnas.
continually	we may feel.	

Léctio Epístolae beáti Pauli Apóstoli ad Corínthios

Fratres:	Ego	enim	accépi	a	Dómino	quod	et
Brothers:	I	indeed	received	from	the Lord	what	also

trádidi	vobis,	quóniam	Dóminus	Jesus,	in	qua
I have given	to you,	that	the Lord	Jesus,	on	the

nocte	tradebátur,	accépit	panem,	et	grátias	agens,
night	he was betrayed,	took	bread,	and	thanks	giving,

---

* This would be a good prayer to learn by heart for Communion. It is the one used at Benediction.

fregit, **et** **dixit:** **Accípite,** **et** **manducáte:** **hoc** **est**
broke, and said: Receive and eat: This is

Corpus **meum** **quod** **pro** **vobis** **tradétur:** **hoc**
Body my which for you shall be delivered, this

fácite **in** **meam** **commemoratiónem.** **Simíliter** **et**
do for my commemoration. In the same way also

cálicem **postquam** **cenávit,** **dicens:** **Hic** **calix**
the chalice, after he dined, saying: This chalice

novum **Testaméntum** **est** **in** **meo** **sánguine.** **Hoc** **fácite,**
the new Testament is in my blood. This do,

quotiescúmque **bibétis,** **in** **meam** **commemoratiónem.**
as often as you shall drink, for my commemoration.

Quotiescúmque **enim** **manducábitis** **panem** **hunc** **et**
As often as, then you eat bread this and

cálicem **bibétis,** **mortem** **Dómini** **annuntiábitis,** **donec**
chalice drink, the death of the Lord you announce, until

véniat. **Itaque,** **quicúmque** **manducáverit** **panem**
he comes. Therefore, whoever eats bread

hunc **vel** **bíberit** **cálicem** **Dómini** **indígne,** **reus**
this or drinks the chalice of the Lord unworthily, guilty

erit **córporis** **et** **sánguinis** **Dómini.** **Probet**
will be of the body and blood of the Lord. Let prove,

autem **seípsum** **homo:** **et** **sic** **de** **pane** **illo** **edat**
then, himself a man: and thus of bread that let him eat

et **de** **cálice** **bibat.** **Qui** **enim** **mandúcat**
and of the chalice let him drink. Who therefore eats

et **bibit** **indígne,** **judícium** **sibi** **mandúcat**
and drinks unworthily, judgment to himself eats

et **bibit:** **non** **dijúdicans** **corpus** **Dómini.**
and drinks, not discerning the body of the Lord.

Graduále

Óculi **ómnium** **in** **te** **sperant,** **Dómine:**
The eyes of all in you hope, Lord:

et	tu	das	illis	escam	in	témpore	opportúno.
and	you	give	them	food	at	the time	suitable.

Aperis	tu	manum	tuam:	et	imples	omne	ánimal
Open	you	hand	your	and	you fill	every	creature

benedictióne.   Alleluía, Alleluía.
with blessing.

Caro	mea	vere	est	cibus,	et	sánguis	meus	vere
Flesh	my	truly	is	food,	and	blood	my	truly

est	potus:	qui	mandúcat	meam	carnem	et	bibit
is	drink.	Who	eats	my	flesh	and	drinks

meum	sánguinem	in	me	manet	et	ego	in	eo.
my	blood	in	me	remains	and	I	in	him.

Sequéntia

[1]Lauda,   Sion,   Salvatórem,
   Praise,   Sion,   the Savior,

Lauda	ducem	et	pastórem
praise	the leader	and	shepherd

In	hymnis	et	cánticis.
in	hymns	and	songs.

———

Quantum[2]	potes,	tantum	aude:
How much	you can,	so much	dare:

Quia	major	omni	laude,
for (He is)	greater	than all	praise,

Nec	laudáre	súfficis.
nor	to praise	do you suffice.

———

Laudis	thema	speciális,
Of praise	the theme	special,

Panis	vivus	et	vitális
the Bread	living	and	vital

* These literal translations, especially of hymns, are not designed to make good English sense apart from the Latin. You can refer to the verse-translations in your Missal for a more adequate English rendering, though no English can approach the amazing combination of poetry, devotion and theology—sound and sense—that St.Thomas Aquinas has achieved in this hymn and the Pange Lingua.

[2] Notice the apposition of **quantum** ... **tantum**. 'How much ... so much ...'

Hódie   propónitur.
today   is proposed.

Quem   in   sacrae   mensa   cenae
Which   on   of the holy   table   supper

Turbae   fratrum   duodénae
to the crowd   of brothers   twelve

Datum   non   ambígitur.
was given   not   it is doubtful.

Sit   laus   plena,   sit   sonóra,
Let be   praise   full,   let it be   sounding,

Sit   jucúnda,   sit   decóra
be   joyful,   be   becoming

Mentis   jubilátio.
of mind   the rejoicing.

Dies   enim   sollémnis   ágitur,*
The day   indeed   solemn   is celebrated,

In   qua   mensae   prima   recólitur
in   which   of table   first   is commemorated

Hujus   institútio.
of this   the institution.

In   hac   mensa,   novi   Regis,
At   this   table,   of the new   King,

Novum   Pascha   novae   legis
the new   Pasch   of the new   law

Phase   vetus   términat.
Pasch   old   ends.

Vetustátem   nóvitas,
The old   the new,

---

* **Agere** is one of those useful verbs which can be used in various contexts
to mean different things, like our 'to do.' It may be equivalent to 'to do,'
'to act,' 'to celebrate,' and in **gratias agere**, 'to give thanks.'

Umbram   fugat   véritas
shadow   puts to flight   truth

Noctem   lux   elíminat.
night   light   eliminates.

Quod   in   cena   Christus   gessit
What   at   table   Christ   did

Faciéndum   hoc   expréssit
to be done   this   he commanded

In   sui   memóriam.
in   of him   the memory.

Docti   sacris   institútis,
Taught   by holy   institutions,

Panem,   vinum   in   salútis
bread,   wine   into   of salvation

Consecrámus   hóstiam.
we consecrate   the Victim.

Dogma   datur   Christiánis
The dogma   is given   to Christians

Quod   in   carnem   transit   panis
that   into   flesh   changes   the bread

Et   vinum   in   sánguinem.
and   the wine   into   blood.

Quod   non   capis,   quod   non   vides,
What   not   you understand,   what   not   you see,

Animósa   firmat   fides,
lively   confirms   faith

Praeter   rerum   órdinem.
above   of things   the order.

Sub   divérsis   speciébus,
Under   different   species

Signis   tantum,   et   non   rebus,
in signs   only,   and   not   in things,

Latent	res	exímiae.
hide	things	wondrous.

Caro	cibus,	sanguis	potus,
Flesh	is food,	blood	is drink,

Manet	tamen	Christus	totus
remains	yet	Christ	whole

Sub	utráqua	spécie.
under	each	species.

A	suménte	non	concísus
By	taking	not	cut

Non	confráctus,	non	divísus,
not	broken,	not	divided,

Ínteger	accípitur.
whole	He is received.

Sumit	unus,	sumunt	mille:
Receives	one,	receive	a thousand:

Quantum	isti,	tantum	ille:
as much as	they,	so much	he,

Nec	sumptus	consúmitur.
nor	having been taken	is it consumed.

Sumunt	boni,	sumunt	mali,
Receive	the good,	receive	the bad,

Sorte	tamen	inaequáli,
in lot	yet	unequal,

Vitae	vel	intéritus.
of life	or	of death.

Mors	est	malis,	vita	bonis:
Death	is	to the bad,	life	to the good:

Vide,	paris	sumptiónis
See,	of like	reception

Quam	sit	dispar	éxitus.
how	may be	different	the result.

131

Fracto		demum	sacraménto,
Having been broken		then	the sacrament,

Ne	vacílles,	sed	meménto,
do not	hesitate,	but	remember

Tantum	esse	sub	fragménto,
as much	is	in	a fragment,

Quantum	toto		tégitur.
as	in the whole		is hidden.

Nulla	rei	fit	scissúra:
Nothing	of the thing	is made	a division,

Signi	tantum	fit	fractúra:
of the sign	only	is	a breaking:

Qua	nec	status	nec	statúra
by which	neither	state	nor	the stature

Signáti		minúitur.
of that signified		is diminished.

Ecce	panis	Angelórum,
See	the bread	of Angels,

Factus	cibus	viatórum,
made	the food	of wayfarers

Vere	panis	filiórum,
truly	bread	of sons,

Non	mitténdus	cánibus.
not	to be given	to dogs.

In	figúris	praesignátur,
In	types	is pre-figured,

Cum	Isaac	immolátur:
when	Isaac	is immolated,

Agnus	Paschae	deputátur,
the Lamb	of the Pasch	is sacrificed,

Datur	manna	pátribus.
given is	manna	to the fathers.

Bone   pastor,   panis   vere,
Good   shepherd,   bread   true,

Jesu,   nostri   miserére,
Jesus,   on us   have mercy,

Tu   nos   pasce,   nos   tuére
You   us   feed,   us   protect,

Tu   nos   bona   fac   vidére
You   us   good things   make   to see

In   terra   vivéntium.
in   the land   of the living.

———

Tu   qui   cuncta   scis   et   vales,
You   who   all things   know   and   can do,

Qui   nos   pascis   hic   mortáles:
Who   us   feed   here   as mortals,

Tuos   ibi   commensáles,
Your   there   table-companions

Coherédes   et   sodáles
co-heirs   and   companions,

Fac   sanctórum   cívium.   Amen.   Alleluia.
make   of the holy   citizens.

Sequéntia Sancti Evangélii secúndum Joánnem

In   illo   témpore: Dixit   Jesus   turbis   Judaeórum:
At   that   time: Said   Jesus   to the crowds   of the Jews:

Caro   mea   vere   est   cibus   et   sanguis   meus   vere
Flesh   my   truly   is   food   and   blood   my   truly

est   potus.   Qui   mandúcat   meam   carnem   et   bibit
is   drink.   Who   eats   my   flesh   and   drinks

meum   sánguinem,   in   me   manet   et   ego   in   illo.
my   blood,   in   me   remains   and   I   in   him.

Sicut   misit   me   vivens   Pater,   et   ego   vivo   propter
As   sent   me   the living   Father,   and   I   live   because

Patrem: et   qui   mandúcat   me,   et   ipse   vivet
of the Father,   so   he who   eats   me,   also   he   will live

133

propter	me.	Hic	est	panis	qui	de	caelo
because of	me.	This	is	the bread	which	from	heaven

descéndit.	Non	sicut	manducavérunt	patres	vestri
came down.	Not	as	ate	fathers	your

manna,	et	mórtui	sunt.	Qui*	mandúcat	hunc
manna,	and	dead	are.	Whoever	eats	this

panem,	vivet	in	aetérnum.
bread,	shall live	into	eternity.

Offertorium

Sacerdótes	Dómini	incénsum	et	panes	ófferunt	Deo:
The priests	of the Lord	incense	and	loaves	offer	to God:

et	ídeo	sancti	erunt	Deo	suo,	et
and	therefore	holy	they shall be	to God	their,	and

non	pólluent	nomen	ejus.	Alleluía.
not	shall defile	name	his.	

Secreta

Ecclésiae	tuae,	quáesumus,	Dómine,	unitátis	et	pacis
To Church	your,	we ask,	Lord,	of unity	and	peace

propítius	dona	concéde:	quae	sub	oblátis
propitiously	the gifts	grant,	which	under	the offered

munéribus	mýstice	designántur.	Per Dóminum nostrum.
gifts	mystically	are designated.	

Communio

Quotiescúmque manducábitis panem hunc et cálicem bibétis, mortem Dómini annuntiábitis, donec véniat: ítaque, quicúmque manducáverit panem vel bíberit cálicem Dómini indígne, reus erit córporis et sánguinis Dómini, Alleluía.

Postcommunio

Fac	nos,	quáesumus,	Dómine,	divinitátis	tuae
Make	us,	we ask,	Lord,	of divinity	your

* Qui frequently has this indefinite meaning of 'whoever'.

sempitérna	fruitióne	repléri:	quam	pretiósi
with the eternal	fruition	to be filled:	which	of precious

Córporis	et	Sánguinis	túi	temporális	percéptio
Body	and	Blood	Your	the temporal	reception

praefigúrat.   **Qui vivis et regnas.**
prefigures.

IN ANNIVERSARIO DEFUNCTORUM

Introitus

Réquiem **aetérnam** **dona** **eis,** **Dómine,** **et** **lux**
Rest eternal give them, Lord, and light

perpétua **lúceat** **eis.** **Te** **decet** **hymnus,** **Deus,**
perpetual let shine on them. You becomes a hymn, God,

in Sion, **et** **tibi** **reddétur** **votum** **in** **Jerúsalem:**
in Sion, and to you will be paid a vow in Jerusalem:

exaúdi **oratiónem** **meam,** **ad** **te** **omnis** **caro** **véniet.**
hear prayer my, to You all flesh shall come.

Réquiem aetérnam, etc.

Orátio

Deus, **indulgentiárum** **Dómine:** **da** **ánimae** **fámuli***
God, of kindnesses Lord: give to the soul of servant

tui **N.** **cujus** **anniversárium** **depositiónis** **diem**
your N. whose anniversary of burial day

commemorámus, **refrigérii** **sedem,** **quiétis**
we commemorate, of refreshment a place, of quiet

beatitúdinem **et** **lúminis** **claritátem.** **Per Dóminum.**
the blessedness and of light the brightness.

Léctio libri Machabraeórum

In **diébus** **íllis:** **Vir** **fortíssimus** **Judas,**
In days those: The man most strong Judas,

facta **collatióne,** **duódecim** **mília** **drachmas**
having been made a collection, twelve thousand drachmas

argénti **misit** **Jerusólymam,** **offérri** **pro** **peccátis**
of silver sent to Jerusalem, to be offered for the sins

mortuórum **sacrifícium,** **bene** **et** **religióse** **de**
of the dead a sacrifice, well and religiously concerning

resurrectióne **cógitans** **(nisi** **enim** **eos,** **qui**
the resurrection thinking (unless for them, who

---

* This is given in the feminine 'famulae', if the Mass is said for a woman, or
the plural: 'famulorum' or 'famularum', or both, if it is said for several people.
This is done also in the Secret and Post-Communion prayers.

cecíderant,	resurrectúros	speráret,	supérfluum
had fallen	to rise again	he had hoped,	superfluous

viderétur		et	vanum	oráre	pro	mórtuis),
it would have seemed		and	vain	to pray	for	the dead),

et	quia	considerábat	quod	hi,	qui	cum	pietáte
and	because	he considered	that	they,	who	with	godliness

dormitiónem	accéperant,	óptimam	habérent	repósitam
sleep	had received,	the best	had	stored up

grátiam.	Sancta	ergo	et	salúbris	est	cogitátio
grace.	Holy	therefore	and	healthful	is	the thought

pro	defúnctis	exoráre,	ut	a	peccátis
for	the dead	to pray,	that	from	sins

solvántur.
they should be loosed.

Graduále

Réquiem aetérnam dona eis, Dómine, et lux perpétua lúceat eis.

In	memória	aetérna	erit	justus,	ab	auditióne
In	memory	eternal	will be	the just man,	from	the hearing

mala	non	timébit.
evil	not	will he fear.

Tractus

Absólve,	Dómine,	ánimas	ómnium	fidélium	defunctórum
Loose,	Lord,	the souls	of all	the faithful	dead

ab	omni	vínculo	delictórum.	Et	grátia	tua	illis
from	all	bond	of sins.	And,	grace	your	them

succurénte,[1]	mereántur	evádere	judícium
helping,	may they merit	escape	the judgment

ultiónis,	et	lucis	aetérnae	beatitúdine
of punishment,	and	the light	of eternal	blessedness

pérfrui.[2]
enjoy (thoroughly).

---

[1] Succurrere — sub + currere, therefore, literally, 'to run under.'
[2] The prefix per, which means 'through' as a preposition, has the sense of 'thorough' in such cases as this.

Dies   irae,   dies   illa
Day   of wrath,   day   that

Solvet   saeclum   in   favílla,
shall dissolve   the world   in   ashes

Teste   David   cum   Sybílla.
by the witness   of David   with   the Sybil.

Quantus   tremor   est   futúrus,
How great   a trembling   is   to be,

Quando   judex   est   ventúrus,
when   the judge   is   to come,

Cuncta   stricte   discussúrus.
everything   with thoroughness   to investigate.

Tuba,   mirum   spargens   sonum
The trumpet,   wonderful   scattering   sound

Per   sepúlchra   regiónum,
through   the graves   of (all) regions,

Coget   omnes   ante   thronum.
shall compel   all   before   the throne.

Mors   stupébit   et   natúra,
Death   will be stunned   and   nature,

Cum   resúrget   creatúra
when   shall rise   the creature

Judicánti   responsúra.
to the judging   to answer.

Liber   scriptus   proferétur,
The book   written   shall be brought,

In   quo   totum   continétur
in   which   everything   is contained

Unde   mundus   judicétur.
whence   the world   shall be judged.

Judex   ergo   cum   sedébit,
The Judge   then   when   he shall sit,

138

Quidquid latet, apparébit,
whatever hides, shall appear,

Nil inúltum remanébit.
nothing unavenged shall remain.

Quid sum miser tunc dictúrus?
What am I poor wretch, then going to say?

Quem patrónum rogatúrus,
whom as a patron call,

Cum vix justus sit secúrus?
when scarcely the just man is secure?

Rex treméndae* majestátis,
King of terrible majesty

Qui salvándos* salvas gratis,
who those to be saved saves freely,

Salva me, fons pietátis.
save me, fountain of kindness.

Recordáre, Jesu pie,
Remember, Jesus kind,

Quod sum causa tuae viae.
that I am the cause of your wayfaring.

Ne me perdas illa die.
do not me destroy on that day.

Quaerens me, sedísti lassus,
Seeking me, you sat weary,

Redemísti Crucem passus:
you redeemed the cross having suffered,

Tantus labor non sit cassus.
so much labor not let be voided.

Juste judex ultiónis,
Just judge of vengeance,

---

* Here are two gerundives, and you will find many more in these hymns. Tremendus literally means 'to be trembled at,' and **salvandos** is used as a noun, 'those to be saved.'

139

Donum   fac   remissiónis
the gift   make   of remission

Ante   diem   ratiónis.
before   the day   of reckoning.

Ingemísco,   tamquam   reus,
I groan,   as   one condemned,

Culpa   rubet   vultus   meus,
guilt   reddens   face   my,

Supplicánti   parce,   Deus.
the suppliant   spare,   God.

Qui   Maríam   absolvísti
You who   Mary   absolved,

Et   latrónem   exaudísti
and   the thief   heard

Mihi   quoque,   spem   dedísti.
to me   also,   hope   have given.

Preces   meae   non   sunt   dignae:
Prayers   my   not   are   worthy:

Sed   tu   bonus   fac   benígne,
but   you   good   do   kindly,

Ne   perénni   cremer   igne.
lest   in eternal I be burned fire.

Inter   oves   locum   praesta,
Among   the sheep a place give,

Et   ab   haedis   me   sequéstra
and   from   the goats me   separate

Státuens   in   parte   dextra.
placing   on   part   right-hand.

Confutátis   maledíctis,
Having been silenced   the wicked,

Flammis   ácribus   addíctis,
to flames   bitter   assigned,

Voca   me   cum   benedíctis.
call   me   with   the blessed.

Oro   supplex   et   acclínis,
I pray   kneeling and   prostrate,

Cor   contrítum quasi   cinis:
my heart   crushed   like   ashes:

Gere   curam   mei   finis.
take   care   of my ending.

Lacrimósa   dies   illa,
Tearful   day   that,

Qua   resúrget   ex   favílla
on which   shall rise from   glowing ashes

Judicándus   homo   reus.
to be judged   man   guilty.

Huic   ergo   parce,   Deus:
Him   then,   spare,   God:

Pie*   Jesu,   Dómine,
kind   Jesus,   Lord,

Dona   eis   réquiem.   Amen.
give   them   rest.

Sequéntia Sancti Evangélii secúndum Joánnem

In   illo   témpore: Dixit   Jesus   turbis   Judaeórum:
At   that   time: said   Jesus   to the crowds   of the Jews:

Omne   quod   dat   mihi   Pater,   ad   me
Everything   which   gives   to me   the Father,   to   me

véniet,   et   eum   qui   venit   ad   me,   non   ejíciam
will come,   and   him   who   comes   to   me,   not   I will throw

foras: quia   descéndi   de   caelo,   non   ut
out,   for   I came down   from   heaven,   not   that

fáciam   voluntátem   meam,   sed   voluntátem   ejus
I should do   will   my,   but   the will   of him

---

* The adjective pius does not mean 'pious' in our sense of the word. It gives the idea of a good relationship between its subject and both God and men. So 'loving', 'kind' or 'good' are better renderings than 'pious', but there is no exact English equivalent.

qui	misit	me.	Haec	est	autem	volúntas	ejus	qui
who	sent	me.	This	is	then	the will	of him	who

misit	me,	Patris:	ut	omne	quod	dedit	mihi,
sent	me,	the Father:	that	all	that	he gave	me,

non	perdam	ex	eo,	sed	resúscitem	illud
not	I should lose	from	it,	but	I again should raise	it

in	novíssimo*	die.	Haec	est	autem	volúntas	Patris
on	the last	day.	This	is	then	the will	of Father

mei,	qui	misit	me:	ut	omnis	qui	videt	Filium
my,	who	sent	me:	that	everyone	who	sees	the Son

et	credit	in	eum,	hábeat	vitam	aetérnam,	et
and	believes	in	him,	may have	life	eternal,	and

ego	resuscitábo	eum	in	novíssimo	die.
I	will raise up	him	on	the last	day.

Offertorium

Dómine	Jesu	Christe,	Rex	glóriae,	líbera	ánimas
Lord	Jesus	Christ,	King	of glory,	free	the souls

ómnium	fidélium	defunctórum	de	poenis	inférni
of all	the faithful	dead	from	the pains	of hell

et	de	profúndo	lacu:	líbera	eas	de	ore
and	from	the deep	lake:	free	them	from	the mouth

leónis,	ne	absórbeat	eas	tártarus,	ne
of the lion,	lest	should swallow	them	Tartarus,	or

cadant	in	obscúrum:	sed	sígnifer	sanctus
they should fall	into	darkness.	But	standard bearer	holy

Míchael	repraeséntet	eas	in	lucem	sanctam:	Quam
Michael	let bring	them	into	light	holy,	which

olim	Ábrahae	promisísti	et	sémini	ejus.
once	to Abraham	you promised	and	to seed	his.

Hóstias	et	preces	tibi,	Dómine,	laudis	offérimus:
Victims	and	prayers	to you,	Lord,	of praise	we offer:

tu	súscipe	pro	animábus	illis,	quárum	hódie
You	take	for	souls	those,	of whom	today

---

* The "last day" in Latin is the novissimus dies, the newest day—which
it certainly will be!

142

memóriam fácimus. Fac eas, Dómine, de morte
memorial we make. Make them, Lord, from death

transíre ad vitam. Quam olim Ábrahae promisísti et
to go across to life.

sémini ejus.

Secreta

Propitiáre, Dómine, supplicatiónibus nostris, pro ánima
Be propitious, Lord, to supplications our, for the soul

fámuli tui N. cujus hódie ánnua dies
of servant your N. whose today anniversary day

ágitur: pro qua tibi offérimus sacrifícium
is celebrated, for which to you we offer sacrifice

laudis; ut eam Sanctórum tuórum consórtio
of praise, that it of Saints your in fellowship

sociáre dignéris. Per Dóminum.
to associate you may deign.

Communio

Lux aetérna lúceat eis: Dómine: Cum Sanctis
Light eternal shine on them, Lord, with saints

tuis in aetérnum: quia pius es. Réquiem
your in eternity, because kind you are.

aetérnam dona eis, Dómine: et lux perpétua lúceat eis. Cum Sánctis
tuis in aetérnum: quia píus es.

Postcommunio

Praesta, quáesumus, Dómine, ut ánima fámuli
Grant, we ask, Lord, that the soul of servant

tui N. cujus anniversárium depositiónis diem
your, N. whose anniversary of burial day

commemorámus: his purgáta sacrifíciis, indulgéntiam
we commemorate, by these purged sacrifices, pardon

páriter et réquiem cápiat sempitérnam. Per
equally and rest may receive eternal.

Dóminum nostrum Jesum Christum.

143

VENI, SANCTE SPIRITUS*

Veni, Sancte Spíritus,
Et emítte coélitus
Lucis tuae rádium.
Veni, pater paúperum,
Veni, dator múnerum,
Veni, lumen córdium.

Consolátor óptime,
Dulcis hospes ánimae,
Dulce refrigérium.
In labóre réquies,
In aestu tempéries,
In fletu solátium.

O lux beatíssima,
Reple cordis íntima
Tuórum fidélium.

Sine tuo númine,
Nihil est in hómine,
Nihil est innóxium.

Lava quod est sórdidum,
Riga quod est áridum,
Sana quod est sáucium.
Flecte quod est rígidum,
Fove quod est frígidum,
Rege quod est dévium.

Da tuis fidélibus,
In te confidéntibus,
Sacrum septenárium,
Da virtútis méritum,
Da salútis éxitum,
Da perénne gaúdium,

Amen, Allelúia.

VENI CREATOR SPIRITUS

Veni Creátor Spíritus,
Mentes tuórum vísita,
Imple supérna grátia
Quae tu creásti péctora.

Qui díceris Paráclitus,
Altíssimi donum Dei,
Fons vivus, ignis, cáritas,
Et spiritális únctio.

Tu, septifórmis múnere,
Dígitus patérnae déxterae,
Tu rite promíssum Patris,
Sermóne dítans gúttura

Accénde lumen sénsibus:
Infúnde ámorem córdibus:
Infírma nostri córporis
Virtúte firmans pérpeti.

Hostem repéllas lóngius,
Pacémque dones prótinus:
Ductóre sic te praevio
Vitémus omne nóxium.

Per te sciámus da Patrem,
Noscámus atque Fílium;
Teque utriúsque Spíritum
Credámus omni témpore.

Deo Patri sit glória,
Et Fílio, qui a mórtuis
Surréxit, ac Paráclito,
In saeculórum saécula.   Amen.

---

* English translations of the following hymns can be found on pages 153-159.

PANGE LINGUA GLORIOSI*

Pange língua gloriósi
Córporis mystérium,
Sanguinísque pretiósi,
Quem in mundi prétium
Fructus ventris generósi
Rex effúdit Géntium.

Nobis datus, nobis natus
Ex intácta Vírgine,
Et in mundo conversátus,
Sparso verbi sémine,
Sui moras incolátus
Miro clausit órdine.

In supréma nocte coenae
Récumbens cum frátribus
Observáta lege plene
Cibis in legálibus,
Cibum turbae duodénae
Se dat suis mánibus.

Verbum caro, panem verum
Verbo carnem éfficit:
Fitque sanguis Christi merum,
Et si sensus déficit,
Ad firmándum cor sincérum
Sola fides súfficit.

Tantum ergo Sacraméntum
Venerémur cérnui:
Et antíquum documéntum
Novo cedat rítui:
Praestet fides suppleméntum
Sénsuum deféctui.

Genitóri, Genitóque
Laus et jubilátio,
Salus, honor, virtus quoque
Sit et benedíctio:
Procedénti ab utróque
Compar sit laudátio.

Amén. Allelúia.

JESU DULCIS MEMORIA

Jesu dulcis memória
Dans vera cordis gaúdia:
Sed super mel et ómnia,
Ejus dulcis praeséntia.

Nil cánitur suávius,
Nil aúditur jucúndius,
Nil cogitátur dúlcius,
Quam Jesus Dei Fílius.

Jesu, spes pœniténtibus,
Quam pius es peténtibus!
Quam bonus te quaeréntibus!
Sed quid inveniéntibus?

Nec língua valet dícere,
Nec líttera exprímere:
Expértus potest crédere,
Quid sit Jesum dilígere.

Sis Jesu nostrum gaúdium,
Qui es futúrus praémium:
Sit nostra in te glória,
Per cuncta semper saécula.

Amen.

---

* The rhythm of the Pange Lingua is said to have been taken from a marching
song of Caesar's Legions. "Ecce, Caésar nunc triúmphat qui subégit Gállias."

STABAT MATER

Stabat Mater dolorósa
Juxta Crucem lacrymósa,
Dum pendébat Fílius.
Cujus ánimam geméntem,
Constristátam et doléntem,
Pertransívit gládius.

O, quam tristis et afflícta
Fúit illa benedícta,
Mater Unigéniti
Quae moerébat et dolébat,
Pia Mater, dum vidébat
Nati poenas ínclyti.

Quis est homo qui non fleret,
Matrem Christi si vidéret
In tanto supplício?
Quis non posset contristári,
Christi Matrem contemplári
Doléntem cum Fílio?

Pro peccátis suae gentis
Vidit Jesum in torméntis,
Et flagéllis súbditum:
Vidit suum dulcem Natum
Moriéndo desolátum,
Dum emísit spíritum.

Eja, Mater, fons amóris
Me sentíre vim dolóris
Fac, ut tecum lúgeam:
Fac, ut árdeat cor meum
In amándo Christum Deum
Ut sibi compláceam.

Sancta Mater, istud agas,
Crucifíxi fige plagas
Cordi meo válide:
Tui Nati vulneráti,
Tam dignáti pro me pati,
Poenas mecum dívide.

Fac me tecum pie flere,
Crucifíxo condolére,
Donec ego víxero:
Juxta Crucem tecum stare,
Et me tibi socíare
In planctu desídero.

Virgo vírginum praeclára,
Mihi jam non sis amára,
Fac me tecum plángere:
Fac, ut portem Christi mortem,
Passiónis fac consórtem,
Et plagas recólere.

Fac me plagis vulnerári,
Fac me Cruce inebriári,
Et cruóre Fílii.
Flammis ne urar succénsus,
Per te, Virgo, sim defénsus
In die judícii.

Christe, cum sit hinc exíre,
Da per Matrem me veníre
Ad palmam victóriae.
Quando corpus moriétur
Fac, ut ánimae donétur
Paradísi glória.

Amen.

JAM LUCIS ORTO SIDERE

Jam lucis orto sídere,
Deum precémur súpplices,
Ut in diúrnis áctibus
Nos servet a nocéntibus.

Linguam refraénans témperet,
Ne litis horror ínsonet,
Visum fovéndo cóntegat,
Ne vanitátes haúriat.

Sint pura cordis íntima,
Absístat et vecórdia:
Carnis terat supérbiam
Potus cibique párcitas.

Ut cum dies abscésserit,
Noctémque sors redúxerit,
Mundi per abstinéntiam
Ipsi canámus glóriam.

Deo Patri sit glória,
Ejúsque soli Fílio,
Cum Spíritu Paráclito,
Nunc et per omne saéculum.
                              Amen.

TE LUCIS ANTE TERMINUM

Te lucis ante términum,
Rerum Creátor, póscimus
Ut pro tua cleméntia
Sis praesul et custódia.

Procul recédant sómnia
Et nóctium phantásmata;
Hostémque nostrum cómprime,
Ne polluántur córpora.

Praesta, Pater piíssime,
Patríque compar Unice,
Cum Spíritu Paráclito
Regnans per omne saéculum.
                              Amen.

147

ALMA REDEMPTORIS MATER

Alma Redemptóris Mater, quae pérvia caeli
Porta manes, et stella maris, succúrre cadénti,
Súrgere qui curat, pópulo: tu quae genuísti,
Natura miránte, tuum sanctum Genitórem,
Virgo prius ac postérius,
Gabriélis ab ore
Sumens illud Ave, peccatórum misérere.

Ángelus Dómini nuntiávit Maríae. Et concépit de Spíritu Sancto.
Orémus: Grátiam tuam, quáesumus, Dómine, méntibus nostris
infúnde: ut, qui Angelo nuntiánte, Christi Fílii túi incarna-
tiónem cognóvimus: per passiónem ejus et crucem, ad resurec-
tiónis glóriam perducámur. Per eúndem Christum Dóminum
nostrum. Amen.

Post partum, Virgo, invioláta permansísti.
Dei Génitrix, intercéde pro nobis.
Orémus: Deus qui salútis aetérnae, beátae Maríae virginitáte foe-
cúnda, humáno géneri praémia praestitísti: tríbue, quaésumus,
ut ipsam pro nobis intercédere sentiámus, per quam merúimus
auctórem vitae suscípere, Dóminum nostrum Jesum Christum,
Fílium tuum. Amen.

AVE, REGÍNA CAELÓRUM

Ave, Regína caelórum,
Ave, Dómina Angelórum:
Salve, radix, salve, porta,
Ex qua mundo lux est orta:

Gaude, Virgo gloriósa,
Super omnes speciósa,
Vale, o valde decóra,
Et pro nobis Christum exóra.

Dignáre me laudáre te, Virgo sacráta
Da mihi virtútem contra hostes tuos.

Orémus: Concéde, miséricors Deus, fragilitáti nostrae praesídium:
ut, qui sanctae Dei Genetrícis memóriam ágimus: intercessiónis
ejus auxílio, a nostris iniquitátibus resurgámus. Per eúndem
Christum Dóminum nostrum. Amen.

REGINA CAELI

Regína caeli, laetáre, allelúia:
Quia quem meruísti portáre, allelúia.
Resurréxit sicut dixit, allelúia.
Ora pro nobis Deum, allelúia.

Gaude et laetáre, Virgo María, Allelúia,
Quia surréxit Dóminus vere, allelúia.

Orémus: Deus qui per resurrectiónem Fílii tui Dómini nostri Jesu
Christi, mundum laetificáre dignátus es: praesta, quaésumus, ut,
per ejus Genitrícem Vírginem Maríam, perpétuae capiámus
gaúdia vitae. Per eúndem Christum Dóminum nostrum. Amen.

SALVE, REGINA

Salve, Regína, mater misericórdiae: vita, dulcédo, et spes nostra,
salve. Ad te clamámus éxsules fílii Hevae. Ad te suspirámus,
geméntes et flentes in hac lacrimárum valle. Eja, ergo, advocáta
nostra, illos tuos misericórdes óculos ad nos convérte. Et Jesum,
benedíctum fructum ventris tui, nobis post hoc exsílium osténde.
O clemens, o pia, o dulcis Virgo María.

Ora pro nobis, sancta Dei Génetrix, ut digni efficiámur promissiónibus Christi.

Orémus: Omnípotens, sempitérne Déus, qui gloriósae Vírginis
Matris Maríae corpus et ánimam, ut dignum Fílii tui habitáculum
éffici mererétur, Spíritu Sancto cooperánte, praeparásti: da, ut
cujus commemoratióne laetámur: ejus pia intercessióne, ab in-
stántibus malis, et a morte perpétua liberémur. Per eúndem
Christum Dóminum nostrum. Amen.

AVE MARIA

Ave, María, grátia plena, Dóminus tecum. Benedícta tu in
muliéribus, et benedíctus fructus ventris tui, Jesu. Sancta María,
Mater Dei, ora pro nobis peccatóribus, nunc et in hora mortis
nostrae. Amen.

LITANY OF LORETTO*

Kyrie, eléison. Christe, eléison. Kyrie, eléison.

Christe, audi nos. Christe, exaúdi nos.

Pater de caelis Deus, miserére nobis.

Fili, Redémptor mundi, Deus, miserére nobis.

Spíritus Sancti Deus, miserére nobis.

Sancta Trínitas, unus Deus, miserére nobis.

Sancta María, ora pro nobis.

Sancta Dei Génitrix, ora pro nobis.

Sancta Virgo vírginum,
Mater Christi,
Mater Divínae grátiae,
Mater puríssima,
Mater castíssima,
Mater inviolata,
Mater intemeráta,
Mater amábilis,
Mater admirábilis,
Mater boni consílii,
Mater Creatóris,
Mater Salvatóris,
Virgo prudentíssima,
Virgo veneránda,
Virgo predicánda,
Virgo potens,
Virgo clemens,
Virgo fidélis,
Speculum justítiae,
Sedes sapiéntiae,
Causa nostra laetítiae,
Vas spirituále,
Vas honorábile,

(ora pro nobis.)

Vas insígne devotiónis,
Rosa mýstica,
Turris Davídica,
Turris ebúrnea,
Domus aúrea,
Fóederis arca,
Jánua caeli,
Stella matutína,
Salus infirmórum,
Refúgium peccatórum,
Consolátrix afflictórum,
Auxílium Christianórum,
Regína angelórum,
Regína patriarchárum.
Regína prophetárum,
Regína apostolórum,
Regína mártyrum,
Regína confessórum,
Regína vírginum,
Regína sanctórum ómnium,
Regína sine labe origináli concépta,
Regína sanctíssimi rosárii,
Regína pacis,

(ora pro nobis.)

Agnus Dei, qui tollis peccáta mundi, parce nobis, Dómine.

Agnus Dei, qui tollis peccáta mundi, exáudi nos, Dómine.

* We are not giving the translation of the Litany, or the two following prayers, because you know it anyway. Notice particularly **amabilis**, 'lovable', rather than the present connotations of 'amiable'; also **veneranda**, and **predicanda**, both gerundives, and meaning 'to be honored', and 'to be praised'. If you have studied any Scholastic Philosophy, you know how much more than our meaning of 'prudent' the author of the Litany meant when he called Our Lady 'Virgo prudentissima',—someone who knew the right thing to do under any circumstances, the right means to take to achieve the right end.

Agnus Dei, qui tollis peccáta mundi, miserére nobis.

Christe, audi nos. Christe, exaúdi nos.

Ora pro nobis, Sancta Dei Génitrix, ut digni efficiámur promissiónibus Christi. Oremus: Concéde nos fámulos tuos, quáesumus, Dómine Deus, perpétua mentis et córporis sanitáte gaudére: et gloriósa beátae Maríae semper Vírginis intercessióne, a praesénte liberári tristítia, et in aeterna pérfrui laetítia. Per Christium Dóminum nóstrum. Amen.

Sub tuum praesídium confúgimus, Sancta Dei Génitrix. Nostras deprecatiónes ne despícias in necessitátibus, sed a periculis cunctis líbera nos semper, Virgo gloriósa et benedícta.

PSALMUS 22

Dóminus regit me, et nihil mihi déerit: in loco páscuae ibi me collocávit.

Super aquam refectiónis educávit me: ánimam meam convértit.

Dedúxit me super sémitas justítiae, propter nomen suum.

Nam, et si ambulávero in médio umbrae mortis, non timébo mala: quóniam tu mecum es.

Virga tua, et báculus tuus: ipsa me consoláta sunt.

Parásti in conspéctu meo mensam, advérsus eos, qui tríbulant me.

Impinguásti in óleo caput meum: et calix meus inébrians quam praeclárus est!

Et misericórdia tua subsequétur me ómnibus diébus vitae meae: Et ut inhábitem in domo Dómini, in longitúdinem diérum.

(The New Psalter of the Roman Breviary, edited and annotated by Rev. L. C. Fillion, S.S., is a wonderful book for explanations of the less obvious parts of the Psalms. It also gives you the Latin of each Psalm on one page and the English on the other, in case you would like more practice with a translation for reference.)

151

PSALMUS 90

(As you see, this Psalm is to be spoken by three people, a narrator, the man who "dwells in the help of the Highest" and the Voice of God.)

Qui hábitat in adjutório Altíssimi, in protectióne Dei caeli commorábitur.

Dicet Dómino: **Suscéptor meus es tu, et refúgium meum: Deus meus sperábo in eum.**

Quóniam ipse liberávit me de láqueo venántium, et a verbo áspero.

Scápulis suis obumbrábit tibi: et sub pennis ejus sperábis.

Scuto circúmdabit te véritas ejus: non timébis a timóre noctúrno.

A sagítta volánte in die, a negótio perambulánte in ténebris: ab incúrsu, et daemónio meridiáno.

Cadent a látere tuo mille, et decem míllia a dextris tuis: ad te autem non appropinquábit.

Verúmtamen óculis tuis considerábis: et retributiónem peccatórum vidébis.

Quóniam tu es, Dómine, spes mea: Altíssimum posuísti refúgium tuum.

Non accédet ad te malum: et flagéllum non appropinquábit tabernáculo tuo.

Quóniam Ángelis suis mandávit de te: ut custódiant te in ómnibus viis tuis.

In mánibus portábunt te: ne forte offéndas ad lápidem pedem tuum.

Super áspidem, et basilíscum ambulábis: et conculcábis leónem et dracónem.

Quóniam in me sperávit, liberábo eum; prótegam eum, quóniam cognóvit nomen meum.

Clamábit ad me, et ego exaúdiam eum: cum ipso sum in tribulatióne: erípiam eum et glorificábo eum.

Longitúdine diérum replébo eum: et osténdam illi salutáre meum.

VENI, SANCTE SPIRITUS

Come, Holy Spirit, and send out the ray of Your heavenly light.
Come, Father of the poor, come, giver of gifts, come, light of hearts.
Best Consoler, sweet guest of the soul, sweet coolness.
In labor, rest; in heat, refreshment; in tears, solace.
O most blessed light, fill the intimate places of the heart of Your faithful.
Without Your power, there is nothing in man, nothing is harmless.
Wash what is soiled, water what is arid, heal what is wounded.
Bend what is rigid, warm what is cold, set right what is wandering.
Give to Your faithful, hoping in You, the holy sevenfold gift,
Give the reward of virtue, give a going out to salvation, give perennial joy. Amen, Alleluia.

VENI, CREATOR SPIRITUS

Come, Creator Spirit, visit the minds of Your Own, fill with heavenly grace the hearts You have created.
You Who are called the Paraclete, the gift of the most high God,
The living fountain, fire, love and spiritual anointing.
You are sevenfold in gift, the finger of the Father's right hand,
You are expressly the promise of the Father, endowing tongues with speech.
Kindle light into our senses, pour love into our hearts, strengthening the weaknesses of the body with perpetual strength.
Drive back the enemy afar, forthwith give peace: so with You leading as a guide, we shall avoid all harm.
Grant that through You we may know the Father, and know also the Son, and may we for all time believe in You, the Spirit of both.
To God the Father be Glory and to the Son, Who rose from the dead, and to the Paraclete, in centuries of centuries. Amen.

PANGE LINGUA

Sing, my tongue, the mystery of the glorious body, and of the precious Blood, which the King of nations, the fruit of a noble womb, poured forth as the price of the world.

Given to us, born for us of a stainless Virgin, and having dwelt in the world, sowing the seed of the word, He closed in a wonderful order the days of His habitation.

On the night of His last supper, reclining with His brothers, the law having been fully observed with legal foods, He gives Himself with His Own hands to the band of twelve.

The Word in Flesh makes true bread His Flesh with a word; wine becomes the Blood of Christ, and if sense is deficient, faith alone is enough to strengthen the sincere heart.

Then let us, prostrate, venerate so great a Sacrament, and let the old law yield to the new rite; let faith stand forward, to supply the defect of the senses.

To the Begetter and the Begotten, be praise and rejoicing, health, honor, and strength: and blessing also, and let equal praise be to Him Who proceeds from Both. Amen, Alleluia.

JESU DULCIS MEMORIA

Jesus, O sweet memory, giving real joys of heart,
But above honey and all things is His sweet presence.

Nothing sweeter is sung, nothing more pleasant is heard, nothing lovelier is thought, than Jesus, the Son of God.

Jesus, hope of penitents, how kind You are to seekers, how good to those asking for You, what, then, to those who find?

Neither tongue is able to say, nor letters to express: he who has experienced can believe what it is to love Jesus.

May You, Jesus, be our joy, Who are to be our reward: May our glory be in You through all the ages always. Amen.

154

STABAT MATER

The sorrowful Mother was standing, tearful, next to the Cross, while her Son was hanging.

Whose groaning soul, broken and sorrowing, the sword pierced.

O, how sad and afflicted was that blessed one, the Mother of the Only-Begotten.

Who grieved and suffered, loving Mother, while she saw the pains of her glorious Son.

Who is the man who would not cry if he saw the Mother of Christ in so great anguish?

Who would be able not to grieve, to contemplate the Mother of Christ sorrowing with her Son?

For the sins of her people, she saw Jesus in torments and subjected to stripes:

She saw her sweet Son, desolate in dying, while He sent out His spirit.

Oh Mother, fountain of love, make me feel the force of sorrow, that I may cry with you,

Make my heart burn in loving Christ, my God, that I may be pleasing to Him.

Holy Mother, may you do this thing: fix the wounds of the Crucified well into my heart,

Divide with me the pains of your wounded Son, Who so deigned to suffer for me.

Make me lovingly weep with you, sorrow with the Crucified as long as I live:

I desire to stand with you next to the Cross and join myself to you in grief.

Most bright Virgin of Virgins, now do not be bitter to me; make me cry with you.

Make me carry the death of Christ, make me a sharer of the Passion and mindful of His wounds.

Make me to be wounded with His wounds, make me drunken with the Cross and Blood of your Son.

Lest I, burned, be consumed by flames, through you, O Virgin, may I be defended in the day of judgment.

Christ, when it is (time) to go away from here, grant that I may come through Your Mother to the palm of victory.

When the body dies, make it so that the glory of Paradise is given to my soul.   Amen.

JAM LUCIS ORTO SIDERE

The star of light now having risen, let us, suppliants, pray God that in our daily acts He may preserve us from harms. Reining it in, may He temper the tongue, lest the horror of quarrel should resound, may He by cherishing, veil our sight lest it draw in vanities.

May the inmost places of the heart be pure, may folly stand away, may scarcity of drink and food wear down the pride of the flesh.

So that when the day has gone away and fate has brought back the night, clean through abstinence, we may sing His glory.

To God the Father be glory, and to His only Son, with the Spirit Paraclete, now and through every age. Amen.

TE LUCIS ANTE TERMINUM

We ask You, Creator of things, before the end of the light, that for Your kindness, You may be a Protector and Guard.

May bad dreams and the phantasms of the night go far away: restrain our enemy lest our bodies should be polluted.

Grant this, most kind Father, and You, the Only Son, Equal to the Father, with the Spirit Paraclete, reigning through all ages. Amen.

ALMA REDEMPTORIS MATER

Kind Mother of the Redeemer, You remain the open door of heaven, and the star of the sea, help your falling people who try to rise: you who, Nature wondering, gave birth to your holy Creator, a Virgin before and after taking that Ave from the mouth of Gabriel, have mercy on sinners.

The Angel of the Lord declared to Mary. And she conceived of the Holy Spirit. Let us pray: O Lord, pour forth Your grace into our minds, we ask: that we who know the incarnation of Christ Your Son, an Angel announcing: through His passion and cross may be led through to the glory of His Resurrection.

After childbirth, O Virgin, you remained inviolate.
Mother of God, intercede for us.

Let us pray. O God who gave to the human race the rewards of eternal life, by the fruitful virginity of blessed Mary: Grant, we ask, that we may know her to intercede for us, through whom we merited to receive the author of life, Our Lord Jesus Christ, Your Son.

AVE, REGINA CAELORUM

Hail, Queen of Heaven, Hail, Lady of Angels: Hail, root, hail, door from which light is arisen to the world:

Rejoice, glorious Virgin, lovely above all. Hail, Oh most beautiful, and pray Christ for us.

Allow me to praise you, holy Virgin. Give me strength against your enemies.

Let us pray: grant, O merciful God, guard of our fragility, that we who celebrate the memory of the holy Mother of God, by the help of her intercession may rise again from our iniquities. Through the same Christ Our Lord.

REGINA CAELI, LAETARE

Queen of heaven, be glad, alleluia. For He whom you merited to bear, alleluia, has risen as He said. Alleluia. Rejoice and be glad, Virgin Mary, alleluia, because the Lord has really risen. Alleluia.

Let us pray: O God Who through the resurrection of Your Son, our Lord Jesus Christ, deigned to gladden the world, grant, we ask, that through His Mother, the Virgin Mary, we may seize the joys of perpetual life. Through the same Christ our Lord. Amen.

SALVE, REGINA

Hail, Queen, Mother of mercy, our life, sweetness and hope, hail! Exiled children of Eve, we clamor to you. To you we sigh, groaning and weeping in this valley of tears. Oh then, our advocate, turn your merciful eyes to us, and after this exile, show us the blessed fruit of your womb, Jesus. O kind, O loving, O sweet Virgin Mary. Pray for us, holy Mother of God, that we may be made worthy of the promises of Christ.

Let us pray: Almighty, eternal God, Who, the Holy Spirit co-operating, prepared the body and soul of the glorious Virgin Mary so that she merited to be made a worthy home for your Son, grant that whose commemoration we rejoice in, by her kind intercession we may be freed from surrounding evils and perpetual death. Through the same Christ our Lord. Amen.

PSALM 90

Who dwells in the help of the Highest, shall abide in the protection of the God of Heaven.

He will say to the Lord, **"You are my guardian and my refuge. My God, I will hope in Him.**

For He has freed me from the trap of the hunters, and from the sharp word."

He will overshadow you with His shoulders, and under His wings shall you hope.

His truth will surround you with a shield, you will not be afraid of the night terror,

Of the arrow flying in the daytime, of the business walking about in the darkness, of an attack, or of the noonday devil.

A thousand shall fall by your side, and ten thousand at your right hand, and it shall not come near you.

Truly with your eyes you will observe and you will see the reward of the wicked.

For you, Lord, are my hope. You have made the Most High your refuge.

Evil will not approach you, and the scourge will not come near your tent.

For He has commanded His angels concerning you, that they may keep you in all your ways.

In their hands they will carry you, lest by chance you should hit your foot against a stone.

You will walk over the viper and the basilisk,* and you will trample on the lion and the dragon.

Since he has hoped in Me, I will deliver him: I will protect him, for he has known my name.

He will cry to me and I will hear him, I am with him in trouble, I will snatch him away and make him glorious.

I will fill him with length of days, and I will show him my salvation.

---

*A basilisk is another unpleasant kind of snake.

The Lord rules me, and nothing is lacking to me; in a place of
pasture, there He has placed me.

Over the water of refreshment he has led me out; he will bring
back my soul.

He has led me over the paths of justice, because of His Name.

For even if I should walk in the middle of the shadow of death,
I will not fear evils, for You are with me.

Your rod and your staff have consoled me.

You have prepared a table in my sight, over against those who
trouble me.

You have anointed my head with oil, and my cheering chalice,
how lovely it is.

And your mercy will follow me for all the days of my life.

So that also I will live in the house of the Lord, into length of days.

Nobody knows exactly how the Romans pronounced their language, but the pronunciation which the Church now uses is that which gives to vowels and consonants approximately the same sounds as they have in modern Italian.

You are used to hearing Latin spoken in the Mass, so that the pronunciation will not seem difficult. Throughout this book, as in most Missals and Breviaries, the syllable on which the accent falls is marked, as **glória,** in all words of more than two syllables. In two syllabled words, the accent always falls on the first.

The Latin alphabet is the same as the English which was borrowed from it, but the Latin does not officially have **J, U** or **W.** You will find any amount of **J's** and **U's** in Latin as now printed. This is because **I** and **V** were originally used as both vowels and consonants, but later it was found clearer to use **J** for the consonant **I,** and **U** for the vowel use of **V.**

Every Latin word has as many syllables as it has vowels or diphthongs, so that each vowel is pronounced separately, except in the case of the diphthongs **ae, oe, au,** each of which make, as it were, one vowel. A final **e** on a word is not mute, but makes another syllable, as **Víde,** "see," pronounced **véeday.**

a English Ah! (long or English of the English **a**): **amo.**

e like the **a** in **fate,** when long: like **e** in **net,** when short: **timēre, concípĕre.**

i like **ee** in **need** when long: like the **i** in **tin** when short: **audīvī, ĭd.**

o as in **no** when long: as in **not** when short: **glōrĭa, nŏn.**

u as in **moon** when long: as in **pull** when short: **ūnitas, ŭt.**

ae and **oe** both like **ay** in **say**: **caelum, poenis.**

au like **ow** in **how**: **laudamus.**

The difference between a long and short vowel lies in the time you take to say it. If you try enunciating the long and short sounds of each vowel as listed above, you will find that you do the same things with your speaking apparatus for both, but you cut the action short in saying a short **e** or **i,** and hold it for a long one.

You will know in general how to pronounce each vowel as you come to it, but the inflected endings on words are apt to be confusing. So in the tables of declensions and conjugations, we have marked the long vowels: **stellīs, amō.**

Every consonant in Latin is sounded.

c is pronounced like **k** before **a, u, au** and **h. caritas, cor, curo, causa, Cherubim.**

c is pronounced as **ch** in cheer, before **e, i, ae** and **oe. Cerno, cibus, caelum** or **coelum.**

g is as in gate, before **a, o, u** and **au. gallus, Goliath, gusto, gaudium.**

g as in **j** in jolly before **e, i** and **ae. gemitus, gigno, gaesum.**

gn is like **ni** in onion. **magnus, lignus.**

sc is as in scatter, before **a, o, u** and **h. scapulae, scopo, scutum, schola.**

sc is as **sh** in wish, before **e, i,** and **ae. ascendo, scindo, scaevus.**

ti, when followed by a vowel is pronounced like **tsi—gratia, benedictio.**

If this should seem difficult think of the way in which 'fish' could be spelled according to the 'rules' of English pronunciation, —**gh** as in enough, **o** as in women, **ti** as in station, **'ghoti'.** Which gives you **fish.** Doesn't it? But if you have any doubts about your Latin pronunciation, ask a priest to read some with you. He will probably be surprised and pleased.

TABLES OF DECLENSION, CONJUGATIONS, ETC.

NOUNS

FIRST DECLENSION

Nom.	stella	*a star*
Gen.	stellae	*of a star*
Dat.	stellae	*to or for a star*
Acc.	stellam	*a star*
Abl.	stellā	*with, from, by, etc., a star*

PLURAL

Nom.	stellae	*stars*
Gen.	stellārum	*of stars*
Dat.	stellīs	*to or for stars*
Acc.	stellās	*stars*
Abl.	stellīs	*with, from, by, etc., stars*

SECOND DECLENSION

Nouns of the Second Declension in **-us,** and **-um,** and in **-er,** and **-ir:**

SINGULAR

	servus, m. slave stem servo-	bellum, n. war stem bello-	puer, m. boy stem puero-	vir, m. man stem viro-
Nom.	servus	bellum	puer	vir
Gen.	servī	bellī	puerī	virī
Dat.	servō	bellō	puerō	virō
Acc.	servum (-om)	bellum	puerum	virum
Abl.	servō	bellō	puerō	virō

PLURAL

Nom.	servī	bella	puerī	virī
Gen.	servōrum	bellōrum	puerōrum	virōrum
Dat.	servīs	bellīs	puerīs	virīs
Acc.	servōs	bella	puerōs	virōs
Abl.	servīs	bellīs	puerīs	virīs

THIRD DECLENSION

CONSONANT STEMS

MUTE STEMS

The whole stem does not appear in the Nominative.

SINGULAR

	radix, f. root stem radic-	rex, m. king stem reg-	cor, n. heart stem cord-
Nom.	rādix	rēx	cor
Gen.	rādīcis	rēgis	cordis
Dat.	rādīcī	rēgī	cordī
Acc.	rādīcem	rēgem	cor
Abl.	rādīce	rēge	corde

PLURAL

Nom.	rādīcēs	rēgēs	corda
Gen.	rādicum	rēgum	cordium
Dat.	rādicibus	rēgibus	cordibus
Acc.	rādicēs	rēgēs	corda
Abl.	rādīcibus	rēgibus	cordibus

LIQUID AND NASAL STEMS (l, n, r)

SINGULAR

	virgo, f. maiden stem virgin-	pater, m. father stem patr-	corpus, n. body stem corpor-
Nom.	virgō	pater	corpus
Gen.	virginis	patris	corporis
Dat.	virginī	patrī	corporī
Acc.	virginem	patrem	corpus
Abl.	virgine	patre	corpore

PLURAL

Nom.	virginēs	patrēs	corpora
Gen.	virginum	patrum	corporum
Dat.	virginibus	patribus	corporibus
Acc.	virginēs	patrēs	corpora
Abl.	virginibus	patribus	corporibus

SINGULAR

	īgnis, m. fire stem **īgni-**	**animal,** n. animal stem **animāli-**
Nom.	īgnis	animal
Gen.	īgnis	animālis
Dat.	īgnī	animālī
Acc.	īgnem	animal
Abl.	īgnī (e)	animālī

PLURAL

Nom.	īgnēs	animālia
Gen.	īgnium	animālium
Dat.	īgnibus	animālibus
Acc.	īgnīs (-es)	animālia
Abl.	īgnibus	animālibus

MIXED i-STEMS

Mixed i-stems are either original i-stems that have lost their i-forms in the singular, or consonant stems that have assumed i-forms in the plural.

SINGULAR

	nūbēs, f. cloud stem **nūb (i)-**	**nox,** f. night stem **noct (i)-**
Nom.	nūbēs	nox
Gen.	nūbis	noctis
Dat.	nūbī	noctī
Acc.	nūbem	noctem
Abl.	nūbe	nocte

PLURAL

Nom.	nūbēs	noctēs
Gen.	nūbium	noctium
Dat.	nūbibus	noctibus
Acc.	nūbīs (-ēs)	noctīs (-ēs)
Abl.	nūbibus	noctibus

167

IRREGULAR NOUNS OF THE THIRD DECLENSION

In many nouns the stem is irregularly modified in the nominative or other cases. Here are a few examples:

SINGULAR

	carō, f. flesh	vis, f. force	iter, n. march
Nom.	carō	vīs	iter
Gen.	carnis	vīs	itineris
Dat.	carnī	vī	itinerī
Acc.	carnem	vim	iter
Abl.	carne	vi	itinere

PLURAL

Nom.	carnēs	virēs	itinera
Gen.	carnium	virium	itinerum
Dat.	carnibus	viribus	itineribus
Acc.	carnēs	virīs (-ēs)	itinera
Abl.	carnibus	viribus	itineribus

FOURTH DECLENSION

The Stem of nouns of the Fourth Declension ends in **u-**. This is usually weakened to **i** before **-bus**. Masculine and Feminine nouns form the nominative by adding **s**; Neuters have for nominative the simple stem, but with **u** (long). Nouns of the Fourth Declension are declined as follows:

manus, f. hand   **genū, n. knee**
stem **manu-**   stem **genu-**

SINGULAR

Nom.	manus	genū
Gen.	manūs	genūs
Dat.	manuī (-ū)	genū
Acc.	manum	genū
Abl.	manū	genū

PLURAL

Nom.	manūs	genua
Gen.	manuum	genuum
Dat.	manibus	genibus
Acc.	manūs	genua
Abl.	manibus	genibus

168

Domus, f. house, has two stems, one ending in **u-** (Fourth Declension) and one ending in **o,** (Second Declension). Hence it shows forms of both the fourth and second declensions:

	SINGULAR	PLURAL
Nom.	domus	domūs
Gen.	domūs (domī)	domuum (domōrum)
Dat.	domuī (domō)	domibus
Acc.	domum	domūs (domōs)
Abl.	domō (domū)	domibus

FIFTH DECLENSION (e-STEMS)

The stem of nouns of the Fifth Declension ends in **ē-,** which appears in all the cases. The Nominative is formed from the stem by adding **s.**

rēs, f. thing   diēs, m. day
stem rē-   stem diē-

SINGULAR

Nom.	rēs	diēs
Gen.	reī	diēī (diē)
Dat.	reī	diēī (diē)
Acc.	rem	diem
Abl.	rē	diē

PLURAL

Nom.	rēs	diēs
Gen.	rērum	diērum
Dat.	rēbus	diēbus
Acc.	rēs	diēs
Abl.	rēbus	diēbus

ADJECTIVES

(a- and o- stems) are declined in the Masculine like **servus, puer** or **ager**; in the Feminine like **stella**; and in the Neuter like **bellum**.

The regular type of an adjective of the First and Second Declensions is declined as follows:

	Masculine stem **bono-**	Feminine stem **bonā-**	Neuter stem **bono-**
		SINGULAR	
Nom.	bonus	bona	bonum
Gen.	bonī	bonae	bonī
Dat.	bonō	bonae	bonō
Acc.	bonum	bonam	bonum
Abl.	bonō	bonā	bonō
		PLURAL	
Nom.	bonī	bonae	bona
Gen.	bonōrum	bonārum	bonōrum
Dat.	bonīs	bonīs	bonīs
Acc.	bonōs	bonās	bona
Abl.	bonīs	bonīs	bonīs

The following adjective with its compounds has the Genitive Singular in **-ius** and the Dative in **-i** in all genders. The Plural of such adjectives is exactly like that of **bonus**. The Singular is thus declined:

unus—one

	m	f	n
Nom.	ūnus	ūna	ūnum
Gen.	ūnīus	ūnīus	ūnīus
Dat.	ūnī	ūnī	ūnī
Acc.	ūnum	ūnam	ūnum
Abl.	ūnō	ūnā	ūnō

Adjectives with three and two terminations are declined as follows:

ācer, ācris, ācre, keen   levis, light
stem ācri-   stem levi-

SINGULAR

	m	f	n	m. f.	n
Nom.	ācer	ācris	ācre	levis	leve
Gen.	ācris	ācris	ācris	levis	levis
Dat.	ācrī	ācrī	ācrī	levī	levī
Acc.	ācrem	ācrem	ācre	levem	leve
Abl.	ācrī	ācrī	ācrī	levī	levī

PLURAL

	m	f	n	m. f.	n
Nom.	ācrēs	ācrēs	ācria	levēs	levia
Gen.	ācrium	ācrium	ācrium	levium	levium
Dat.	ācribus	ācribus	ācribus	levibus	levibus
Acc.	ācrīs (-ēs)	ācrīs (-ēs)	ācria	levīs (-ēs)	levia
Abl.	ācribus	ācribus	ācribus	levibus	levibus

Adjectives with one termination are declined as follows:

par, equal: stem par-

	SINGULAR		PLURAL	
	m. f.	n	m. f.	n
Nom.	pār	pār	parēs	paria
Gen.	paris	paris	parium	parium
Dat.	parī	parī	paribus	paribus
Acc.	parem	par	parīs (-ēs)	paria
Abl.	parī	parī	paribus	paribus

DECLENSION OF COMPARATIVES

melior, better   **plūs,** more
stem **melior-**   stem **plūr-**

SINGULAR

	m-f	n	m-f	n
Nom.	melior	melius	......	plūs
Gen.	meliōris	meliōris	......	plūris
Dat.	meliōrī	meliōrī	......	.....
Acc.	meliōrem	melius	......	plūs
Abl.	meliōre (-i)	meliōre (-i)	......	plūre

PLURAL

	m-f	n	m-f	n
Nom.	meliōrēs	meliōra	plūrēs	plūra
Gen.	meliōrum	meliōrum	plūrium	plūrium
Dat.	meliōribus	meliōribus	plūribus	plūribus
Acc.	meliōrēs (-īs)	meliōra	plūrēs (-īs)	plūra
Abl.	meliōribus	meliōribus	plūribus	plūribus

IRREGULAR COMPARISON

bonus, good	melior, better	optimus, best
malus, bad	peior, worse	pessimus, worst
māgnus, great	maior, greater	maximus, greatest
parvus, small	minor, less	minimus, least
multus, much	plus, more (a noun)	plurimus, most
multi, many	plures, more	plurimi, most
nequam, worthless	nequior	nequissimus

PRONOUNS

PERSONAL PRONOUNS

FIRST PERSON

	SINGULAR	PLURAL
Nom.	ego, *I*	nōs, *we*
Gen.	meī, *of me*	nostrum, nostrī, *of us*
Dat.	mihi, *to me*	nōbīs, *to us*
Acc.	mē, *me*	nōs, *us*
Abl.	mē, *by me*	nōbīs, *by us*

SECOND PERSON

Nom.	tū, *thou, you*	vōs, *ye or you*
Gen.	tuī, *of thee, you*	vestrum, vestrī; vostrum (-trī), *of you.*
Dat.	tibi, *to thee, to you*	vōbīs, *to you*
Acc.	tē, *thee, you*	vōs, *you*
Abl.	tē, *by thee, by you*	vōbīs, *by you*

POSSESSIVE PRONOUNS

First Person	meus, *my*	noster, *our*
Second Person	tuus, *thy, your*	vester, *your*
Third Person	suus, *his, her, its*	suus, *their*

DEMONSTRATIVE PRONOUNS

hīc, this

	SINGULAR			PLURAL		
	m	f	n	m	f	n
Nom.	hīc	haec	hōc	hī	hae	haec
Gen.	hūius	hūius	hūius	hōrum	hārum	hōrum
Dat.	huic	huic	huic	hīs	hīs	hīs
Acc.	hunc	hanc	hōc	hōs	hās	haec
Abl.	hōc	hāc	hōc	hīs	hīs	hīs

is, that

	m	f	n	m	f	n
Nom.	is	ea	id	eī, īī	eae	ea
Gen.	eius	eius	eius	eōrum	eārum	eōrum
Dat.	eī	eī	eī	eīs, īīs (īs)	eīs, īīs (īs)	eīs, īīs (īs)
Acc.	eum	eam	id	eōs	eās	ea
Abl.	eō	eā	eō	eīs, īīs	eīs, īīs	eīs, īīs

ille, that

Nom.	ille	illa	illud	illī	illae	illa
Gen.	illīus	illīus	illīus	illōrum	illārum	illōrum
Dat.	illī	illī	illī	illīs	illīs	illīs
Acc.	illum	illam	illud	illōs	illās	illā
Abl.	illō	illā	illō	illīs	illīs	illīs

iste, ista, istud, 'that'—is declined like ille

idem, the same

Nom.	īdem	eadem	idem	īdem (ei-)	eaedem	eadem
Gen.	eiusdem	eiusdem		eōrundem	eārundem	
			eiusdem			eōrundem
Dat.	eīdem	eīdem	eīdem	eīsdem or īsdem		
Acc.	eundem	eandem	idem	eōsdem	eāsdem	eadem
Abl.	eōdem	eādem	eōdem	eīsdem or īsdem		

INTENSIVE PRONOUN

ipse, self

Nom.	ipse	ipsa	ipsum	ipsī	ipsae	ipsa
Gen.	ipsīus	ipsīus	ipsīus	ipsōrum	ipsārum	ipsōrum
Dat.	ipsī	ipsī	ipsī	ipsīs	ipsīs	ipsīs
Acc.	ipsum	ipsam	ipsum	ipsōs	ipsās	ipsā
Abl.	ipsō	ipsā	ipsō	ipsīs	ipsīs	ipsīs

RELATIVE PRONOUNS

Nom.	quī	quae	quod	quī	quae	quae
Gen.	cūius	cūius	cūius	quōrum	quārum	quōrum
Dat.	cui	cui	cui	quibus	quibus	quibus
Acc.	quem	quam	quod	quōs	quās	quae
Abl.	quō	quā	quō	quibus	quibus	quibus

INTERROGATIVE PRONOUNS

Nom.	quis	quid	
Gen.	cūius	cūius	The plural is the same as that of the
Dat.	cui	cui	relative pronoun.
Acc.	quem	quid	
Abl.	quō	quō	

INDEFINITE PRONOUNS

	m	f	n
Nom.	aliquis (aliqui)	aliqua	aliquid (aliquod)
Gen.	alicūius	alicūius	alicūius
Dat.	alicui	alicui	alicui
Acc.	aliquem	aliquam	aliquid (aliquod)
Abl.	aliquō	aliquā	aliquō

PLURAL

Nom.	aliquī	aliquae	aliqua
Gen.	aliquōrum	aliquārum	aliquōrum
Dat.	aliquibus	aliquibus	aliquibus
Acc.	aliquōs	aliquās	aliqua
Abl.	aliquibus	aliquibus	aliquibus

───────────────

CONJUGATION OF THE VERB

The verb **esse,** to be, is both irregular and defective.

Principal Parts: Present Indicative, **sum,** Present Infinitive, **esse,** Perfect Indicative, **fuī,** Future Participle, **futūrus.**

Present Stem **es-**   Perfect Stem **fu-**   Supine Stem **fut-**

INDICATIVE   SUBJUNCTIVE

PRESENT

	INDICATIVE	SUBJUNCTIVE
Sing. 1.	**sum,** *I am*	sim
2.	**es,** *thou art (you are)*	sīs
3.	**est,** *he (she, it) is*	sit
Plur. 1.	**sumus,** *we are*	sīmus
2.	**estis,** *you are*	sītis
3.	**sunt,** *they are*	sint

IMPERFECT

	INDICATIVE	SUBJUNCTIVE
Sing. 1.	**eram,** *I was*	essem
2.	**erās,** *you were*	essēs
3.	**erat,** *he (she, it) was*	esset
Plur. 1.	**erāmus,** *we were*	essēmus
2.	**erātis,** *you were*	essētis
3.	**erant,** *they were*	essent

FUTURE*

	INDICATIVE
Sing. 1.	**erō,** *I shall be*
2.	**eris,** *you will be*
3.	**erit,** *he will be*
Plur. 1.	**erimus,** *we shall be*
2.	**eritis,** *you will be*
3.	**erunt,** *they will be*

PERFECT

	INDICATIVE	SUBJUNCTIVE
Sing. 1.	**fuī,** *I was (have been)*	fuerim
2.	**fuistī,** *you were*	fuerīs
3.	**fuit,** *he was*	fuerit
Plur. 1.	**fuimus,** *we were*	fuerīmus
2.	**fuistis,** *you were*	fuerītis
3.	**fuērunt, fuēre,** *they were*	fuerint

---

* There is no Future Subjunctive in Latin. *No* verb has it.

INDICATIVE	SUBJUNCTIVE

PLUPERFECT

Sing.	1. **fueram,** *I had been*	**fuissem**
	2. **fuerās,** *you had been*	**fuissēs**
	3. **fuerat,** *he had been*	**fuisset**
Plur.	1. **fuerāmus,** *we had been*	**fuissēmus**
	2. **fuerātis,** *you had been*	**fuissētis**
	3. **fuerant,** *they had been*	**fuissent**

FUTURE PERFECT

Sing. 1. **fuerō,** *I shall have been*
     2. **fueris,** *you will have been*
     3. **fuerit,** *he will have been*
Plur. 1. **fuerimus,** *we shall have been*
     2. **fueritis,** *you will have been*
     3. **fuerint,** *they will have been*

IMPERATIVE

	Sing.	Plural
Present	**es,** *be thou*	**este,** *be ye*
Future	**estō,** *thou shalt be*	**estōte,** *ye shall be*
	estō, *he shall be*	**suntō,** *they shall be*

INFINITIVE

Present	**esse,** *to be*
Perfect	**fuisse,** *to have been*
Future	**futūrus esse** or **fore,** *to be about to be*

PARTICIPLE

Future	**futūrus, -a, -um,** *about to be*

Principal Parts: Present Indicative, **amō,** Present Infinitive, **amāre,**
Perfect Indicative, **amāvī,** Perfect Passive Participle, **amātus.**

Present Stem—**ama-,** Perfect Stem—**amav-,** Supine Stem—**amat-**

INDICATIVE	SUBJUNCTIVE
(statements)	(hopes, wishes, purposes.)

PRESENT

amō,[1] *I love, am loving, do love*	**amem**[2]
amās, *you love*	**amēs**
amāt, *he loves*	**amet**
amāmus, *we love*	**amēmus**
amātis, *you love*	**amētis**
amant, *they love*	**ament**

IMPERFECT

amābam, *I was loving*	**amārem**
amābās, *you were loving*	**amārēs**
amābat, *he was loving*	**amāret**
amābāmus, *we were loving*	**amārēmus**
amābātis, *you were loving*	**amārētis**
amābant, *they were loving*	**amārent**

FUTURE

amābō, *I shall love*	
amābis, *you will love*	
amābit, *he will love*	
amābimus, *we shall love*	
amābitis, *you will love*	
amābunt, *they will love*	

PERFECT

amāvī, *I loved*	**amāverim**
amāvistī, *you loved*	**amāverīs**
amāvit, *he loved*	**amāverit**
amāvimus, *we loved*	**amāverīmus**
amāvistis, *you loved*	**amāverītis**
amāvērunt (-ēre), *they loved*	**amāverint**

---

[1] The stem-vowel ā is lost before ō and in the Present Subjunctive becomes ē.
[2] There is no one translation of the Subjunctive (see page 45).

INDICATIVE	SUBJUNCTIVE

PLUPERFECT

amāveram, *I had loved*	amāvissem
amāverās *etc.,*	amāvissēs
amāverat	amāvisset
amāverāmus	amāvissēmus
amāverātis	amāvissētis
amāverant	amāvissent

FUTURE PERFECT

amāverō, *I shall have loved*	amāverimus
amāveris *etc.*	amāveritis
amāverit	amāverint

IMPERATIVE (Commands)

PRESENT	amā, *love (sing.)*	amāte, *love (plural)*
FUTURE	amātō, *thou shalt love*	amātōte, *ye shall love*
	amātō, *he shall love*	amantō, *they shall love*

INFINITIVE

PRESENT	amāre, *to love*
PERFECT	amāvisse or amāsse, *to have loved*
FUTURE	amātūrus esse, *to be about to love*

PARTICIPLES

PRESENT	amāns, -antis, *loving*
FUTURE	amātūrus, -a, -um, *about to love*

GERUND

GENITIVE	amandī, *of loving*	ACCUSATIVE	amandum, *loving*
DATIVE	amandō, *for loving*	ABLATIVE	amandō, *by loving*

SUPINE

amātum, to love amātū, to love

179

FIRST CONJUGATION (a-STEMS)—PASSIVE VOICE

Principal Parts: Present Indicative, **amor,** Present Infinitive, **amārī,**
Perfect Indicative, **amātus sum.**

Present Stem—**amā-**   Supine Stem—**amāt-**

INDICATIVE   SUBJUNCTIVE

PRESENT

amor, *I am loved, being loved*	**amer**
amāris (-re), *you are loved*	**amēris (-re)**
amātur, *he is loved*	**amētur**
amāmur, *we are loved*	**amēmur**
amāminī, *you are loved*	**amēminī**
amantur, *they are loved*	**amentur**

IMPERFECT

amābar, *I was loved, being loved*	**amārer**
amābāris, *you were loved*	**amārēris (-re)**
amābātur, *he was loved*	**amārētur**
amābāmur, *we were loved*	**amārēmur**
amābāminī, *you were loved*	**amārēminī**
amābantur, *they were loved*	**amārentur**

FUTURE

amābor, *I shall be loved*
amāberis (-re), *you will be loved*
amābitur, *we will be loved*
amābimur, *we shall be loved*
amābiminī, *you will be loved*
amābuntur, *they will be loved*

PERFECT

amātus sum, *I was loved*	**amātus sim**
amātus es, *you were loved*	**amātus sīs**
amātus est, *he was loved*	**amātus sīt**
amātī sumus, *we were loved*	**amātī sīmus**
amātī estis, *you were loved*	**amātī sītis**
amātī sunt, *they were loved*	**amātī sint**

INDICATIVE	SUBJUNCTIVE

PLUPERFECT

amātus eram, *I had been loved*	amātus essem
amātus eras *etc.*	amātus essēs
amātus erat	amātus esset
amāti eramus	amātī essēmus
amāti eratis	amātī essētis
amāti erant	amātī essent

FUTURE PERFECT

Singular	Plural
amātus erō, *I shall have been loved*	amāti erimus
amātus eris *etc.*	amātī eritis
amātus erit	amātī erunt

IMPERATIVE

PRESENT	amāre, *be thou loved*	amāminī, *be ye loved*
FUTURE	amātor, *thou shalt be loved*	
	amātor, *he shall be loved*	amantor, *they shall be loved*

INFINITIVE

PRESENT	amārī, *to be loved*
PERFECT	amātus esse, *to have been loved*
FUTURE	amātum īrī, *to be about to be loved*

PARTICIPLES

PERFECT	amātus, -a, -um, *loved*
FUTURE (GERUNDIVE)	amandus, -a, -um, *to be loved*

SECOND CONJUGATION (e-STEMS)

Principal Parts: Active, **moneō, monēre, monuī, monitus,**
Passive, **moneor, monēri, monitus sum.**

Present Stem, **mone-** Perfect Stem, **monu-** Supine Stem, **monit-**

ACTIVE VOICE
INDICATIVE SUBJUNCTIVE

PASSIVE VOICE
INDICATIVE SUBJUNCTIVE

PRESENT

moneō	moneam	moneor	monear
monēs	moneās	monēris (-re)	moneāris (-re)
monet	moneat	monētur	moneātur
monēmus	moneāmus	monēmur	moneāmur
monētis	moneātis	monēminī	moneāminī
monent	moneant	monentur	moneantur

IMPERFECT

monēbam	monērem	monēbar	monērer
monēbās	monērēs	monēbāris (-re)	monērēris (-re)
monēbat	monēret	monēbātur	monērētur
monēbāmus	monērēmus	monēbāmur	monērēmur
monēbātis	monērētis	monēbāminī	monērēminī
monēbant	monērent	monēbantur	monērentur

FUTURE   FUTURE

monēbō	monēbor
monēbis	monēberis (-re)
monēbit	monēbitur
monēbimus	monēbimur
monēbitis	monēbiminī
monēbunt	monēbuntur

PERFECT   PERFECT

monuī	monuerim	monitus sum	monitus sim
monuistī	monueris	monitus es	monitus sīs
monuit	monuerit	monitus est	monitus sīt
monuimus	monuerīmus	monitī sumus	monitī sīmus
monuistis	monuerītis	monitī estis	monitī sītis
monuērunt (-re)	monuerint	monitī sunt	monitī sint

| ACTIVE VOICE | | PASSIVE VOICE | |
| INDICATIVE | SUBJUNCTIVE | INDICATIVE | SUBJUNCTIVE |

PLUPERFECT

monueram	monuissem	monitus eram	monitus essem
monuerās	monuissēs	monitus erās	monitus essēs
monuerat	monuisset	monitus erat	monitus esset
monuerāmus	monuissēmus	monitī erāmus	monitī essēmus
monuerātis	monuissētis	monitī erātis	monitī essētis
monuerant	monuissent	monitī erant	monitī essent

FUTURE PERFECT

monuerō	monitus erō
monueris	monitus eris
monuerit	monitus erit
monuerimus	monitī erimus
monueritis	monitī eritis
monuerint	monitī erunt

IMPERATIVE

	ACTIVE			PASSIVE	
	Singular	Plural		Singular	Plural
PRESENT	monē	monēte	PRESENT	monēre	monēminī
FUTURE	monētō	monētōte	FUTURE	monētor	....
	monētō	monentō		monētor	monentor

INFINITIVE

	ACTIVE	PASSIVE
PRESENT	monēre	monērī
PERFECT	monuisse	monitus esse
FUTURE	monitūrus esse	monitum īrī

PARTICIPLES

	ACTIVE		PASSIVE
PRESENT	monēns, -entis	PERFECT	monitus, -a, -um
FUTURE	monitūrus, -a, -um	GERUNDIVE	monendus, -a, -um

GERUND

monendī, -dō, -dum, -dō

SUPINE

monitum, monitū

183

THIRD CONJUGATION (e-STEMS)*

Principal Parts: Active, **tegō, tegere, tēxī, tēctus,**
Passive, **tegor, tegī, tēctus sum.**

Present Stem **tege-**   Perfect Stem **tex-**   Supine Stem **tēct-**

ACTIVE VOICE		PASSIVE VOICE	
INDICATIVE	SUBJUNCTIVE	INDICATIVE	SUBJUNCTIVE

PRESENT		PRESENT	
tegō	tegam	tegor	tegar
tegis	tegās	tegeris (-re)	tegāris (re)
tegit	tegat	tegitur	tegātur
tegimus	tegāmus	tegimur	tegāmur
tegitis	tegātis	tegiminī	tegāminī
tegunt	tegant	teguntur	tegantur

IMPERFECT		IMPERFECT	
tegēbam	tegerem	tegēbar	tegerer
tegēbās	tegerēs	tegēbāris (-re)	tegerēris (-re)
tegēbat	tegeret	tegēbātur	tegerētur
tegēbāmus	tegerēmus	tegēbāmur	tegerēmur
tegēbātis	tegerētis	tegēbāminī	tegerēminī
tegēbant	tegerent	tegēbantur	tegerentur

FUTURE	FUTURE
tegam	tegar
tegēs	tegēris (-re)
teget	tegētur
tegēmus	tegēmur
tegētis	tegēminī
tegent	tegentur

---

* There are also verbs in -io of the Third Conjugation like **capio, capere, cepi, captus,** which have certain forms of the present stem like the Fourth Conjugation, but if you know the regular third and fourth conjugations, you will have no trouble with them.

184

ACTIVE VOICE
INDICATIVE   SUBJUNCTIVE

PERFECT

tēxī	tēxerim
tēxistī	tēxerīs
tēxit	tēxerit
tēximus	tēxerīmus
tēxistis	tēxerītis
tēxērunt (-re)	tēxerint

PLUPERFECT

tēxeram	tēxissem
tēxerās	tēxissēs
tēxerat	tēxisset
tēxerāmus	tēxissēmus
tēxerātis	tēxissētis
tēxerant	tēxissent

FUTURE PERFECT

tēxerō	
tēxeris	
tēxerit	
tēxerimus	
tēxeritis	
tēxerint	

PASSIVE VOICE
INDICATIVE   SUBJUNCTIVE

PERFECT

tēctus sum	tēctus sim
tēctus es	tēctus sīs
tēctus est	tēctus sit
tēctī sumus	tēctī sīmus
tēctī estis	tēctī sītis
tēctī sunt	tēctī sint

PLUPERFECT

tēctus eram	tēctus essem
tēctus erās	tēctus essēs
tēctus erat	tēctus esset
tēctī erāmus	tēctī essēmus
tēcti erātis	tēctī essētis
tēctī erant	tēctī essent

FUTURE PERFECT

tēctus erō	
tēxtus eris	
tēctus erit	
tēctī erimus	
tēctī eritis	
tēctī erunt	

IMPERATIVE

	ACTIVE		PASSIVE	
	Singular	Plural	Singular	Plural
PRESENT	tege	tegite	tegere	tegiminī
FUTURE	tegitō	tegitōte	tegitor	. . . .
	tegitō	teguntō	tegitor	teguntor

INFINITIVE

	ACTIVE	PASSIVE
PRESENT	tegere	tegī
PERFECT	tēxisse	tēctus esse
FUTURE	tēcturūs esse	tēctum īrī

PARTICIPLES

	ACTIVE		PASSIVE
PRESENT	tegēns, -entis	PERFECT	tēctus, -a, -um
FUTURE	tēctūrus, -a, -um	GERUNDIVE	tegendus (-undus)

GERUND
tegendī, -dō, -dum, -dō

SUPINE
tēctum, tēctū

FOURTH CONJUGATION (i-STEMS)

Principal Parts: Active, audiō, audīre, audīvī, audītus,
Passive, audior, audīrī, auditus sum.

Present Stem, audī-   Perfect Stem, audīu-   Supine Stem, audīt-

ACTIVE VOICE		PASSIVE VOICE	
INDICATIVE	SUBJUNCTIVE	INDICATIVE	SUBJUNCTIVE
PRESENT		**PRESENT**	
audiō	audiam	audior	audiar
audīs	audiās	audīris (-re)	audiāris (-re)
audit	audiat	audītur	audiātur
audīmus	audiāmus	audīmur	audiāmur
audītis	audiātis	audīminī	audiāminī
audiunt	audiant	audiuntur	audiantur
IMPERFECT		**IMPERFECT**	
audiēbam	audīrem	audiēbar	audīrer
audiēbās	audīrēs	audiēbāris (-re)	audīrēris (-re)
audiēbat	audīret	audiēbātur	audīrētur
audiēbāmus	audīrēmus	audiēbāmur	audīrēmur
audiēbātis	audīrētis	audiēbāminī	audīrēminī
audiēbant	audīrent	audiēbantur	audīrentur
FUTURE		**FUTURE**	
audiam		audiar	
audiēs		audiēris (-re)	
audiet		audiētur	
audiēmus		audiēmur	
audiētis		audiēminī	
audient		audientur	

186

ACTIVE VOICE

INDICATIVE	SUBJUNCTIVE

PERFECT

audīvī	audīverim
audīvistī	audīverīs
audīvit	audīverit

audīvimus	audīverīmus
audīvistis	audīverītis
audīvērunt (-re)	audīverint

PLUPERFECT

audīveram	audīvissem
audīverās	audīvissēs
audīverat	audīvisset

audīverāmus	audīvissēmus
audīverātis	audīvissētis
audīverant	audīvissent

FUTURE PERFECT

audīverō
audīveris
audīverit

audīverimus
audīveritis
audīverint

PASSIVE VOICE

INDICATIVE	SUBJUNCTIVE

PERFECT

audītus sum	audītus sim
audītus es	audītus sīs
audītus est	audītus sit

audītī sumus	audītī sīmus
audītī estis	audītī sītis
audītī sunt	audītī sint

PLUPERFECT

audītus eram	audītus essem
audītus erās	audītus essēs
audītus erat	audītus esset

audītī erāmus	audītī essēmus
audītī erātis	audītī essētis
audītī erant	audītī essent

FUTURE PERFECT

audītus erō
audītus eris
audītus erit

audītī erimus
audītī eritis
audītī erunt

IMPERATIVE

	ACTIVE		PASSIVE	
	Singular	Plural	Singular	Plural
PRESENT	audī	audīte	audīre	audīminī
FUTURE	audītō	audītōte	audītor	. . . .
	audītō	audiuntō	audītor	audiuntor

INFINITIVE

	ACTIVE	PASSIVE
PRESENT	audīre	audīrī
PERFECT	audīvisse	audītus esse
FUTURE	audītūrus esse	audītum īrī

187

PARTICIPLES

	ACTIVE		PASSIVE
PRESENT	audiēns, -ientis	PERFECT	audītus, -a, -um
FUTURE	audītūrus, -a, -um	GERUNDIVE	audiendus, -a, -um

GERUND

audiendī, -dō, -dum, -dō

SUPINE

audītum, audītū

IRREGULAR VERBS

possum

Principal Parts: **possum, posse, potuī**

	INDICATIVE		SUBJUNCTIVE	
	Singular	Plural	Singular	Plural
Present	possum	possumus	possim	possīmus
	potes	potestis	possīs	possītis
	potest	possunt	possit	possint
Imperfect	poteram	poterāmus	possem	possēmus
Future	poterō	poterimus	......	......
Perfect	potuī	potuimus	potuerim	potuerīmus
Pluperfect	potueram	potuerāmus	potuissem	potuissēmus
Fut. Perf.	potuerō	potuerimus	......	......

INFINITIVE

Pres. **posse**   Perf. **potuisse**

PARTICIPLE

Pres. **potēns**

volō, nōlō, mālō

Principal Parts: **volō, velle, voluī,** ......, *be willing, will wish*
                 nōlō, nōlle, nōluī, ..., *be unwilling, will not*
                 mālō, mālle, māluī, ..., *be more willing, prefer*

INDICATIVE

Present	volō	nōlō	mālō
	vīs	nōn vīs	māvīs
	vult	nōn vult	māvult
	volumus	nōlumus	mālumus
	vultis	nōn vultis	māvultis
	volunt	nōlunt	mālunt
Imperfect	volēbam	nōlēbam	mālēbam
Future	volam, volēs, etc.	nōlam, nōlēs, etc.	mālam, mālēs, etc.
Perfect	voluī	nōluī	māluī
Pluperfect	volueram	nōlueram	mālueram
Fut. Perf.	voluerō	nōluerō	māluerō

SUBJUNCTIVE

Present	velim, -īs, -it	nōlim	mālim
	velīmus, -ītis, -int		
Imperfect	vellem, -ēs, -et	nōllem	māllem
	vellēmus, -ētis, -ent		
Perfect	voluerim	nōluerim	māluerim
Pluperfect	voluissem	nōluissem	māluissem

IMPERATIVE

Present	......	nōlī, nōlīte	......
Future	......	nōlītō, etc.	......

INFINITIVE

Present	velle	nōlle	mālle
Perfect	voluisse	nōluisse	māluisse

PARTICIPLES

Present	volēns, -entis	nōlēns, -entis	......

189

fero, bear, carry, endure

Principal Parts: **ferō, ferre, tuli, lātus**

Present Stem **fer-**   Perfect Stem **tul-**   Supine Stem **lat-**

	ACTIVE		PASSIVE	
		INDICATIVE		
Present	**ferō**	**ferimus**	**feror**	**ferimur**
	fers	**fertis**	**ferris (-re)**	**feriminī**
	fert	**ferunt**	**fertur**	**feruntur**
Imperfect	**ferēbam**		**ferēbar**	
Future	**feram**		**ferar**	
Perfect	**tulī**		**lātus sum**	
Pluperfect	**tuleram**		**lātus eram**	
Fut. Perf.	**tulerō**		**lātus erō**	

SUBJUNCTIVE

Present	**feram**		**ferar**
Imperfect	**ferrem**		**ferrer**
Perfect	**tulerim**		**lātus sim**
Pluperfect	**tulissem**		**lātus essem**

IMPERATIVE

Present	**fer**	**ferte**	**ferre**	**feriminī**
Future	**fertō**	**fertōte**	**fertor**	. . . .
	fertō	**feruntō**	**fertor**	**feruntor**

INFINITIVE

Present	**ferre**		**ferrī**
Perfect	**tulisse**		**lātus esse**
Future	**lātūrus esse**		**lātum īrī**

PARTICIPLES

Present	**ferēns, -entis**	Perfect	**lātus**
Future	**lātūrus**	Gerundive	**ferendus**

GERUND	SUPINE
ferendī, -dō, -dum, -dō	**lātum, lātū**

190

Eo, go

Principal Parts: **eō, īre, iī (īvī), itum.**

	INDICATIVE	SUBJUNCTIVE
Present	**eō, īs, it**	**eam, eās, eat**
	īmus, ītis, eunt	**eāmus, eātis, eant**
Imperfect	**ībam, ībās, ībat**	**īrem, īres, īret**
	ībāmus, ībātis, ībant	**īrēmus, īrētis, īrent**
Future	**ībō, ībis, ībit**	
	ībimus, ībitis, ībunt	
Perfect	**iī (īvī)**	**ierim (īverim)**
Pluperfect	**ieram (īveram)**	**īssem (īvissem)**
Fut. Perf.	**ierō (īverō)**	

IMPERATIVE

Present	**ī**		Future	**ītō, ītōte**
	īte			**ītō, euntō**

INFINITIVE

Present **īre**   Perfect **īsse (īvisse)**   Future **itūrus esse**

PARTICIPLES

Present **iēns**, gen. **euntis**   Future **itūrus**   Gerundive **eundum**

GERUND	SUPINE
eundī, -dō, -dum, -dō	**itum, itū**

Facio, facere, feci, factum, *make,* is regular, but it has imperative **fac** in the active. The passive of **facio** is—**fīō, fīerī, factus sum,** be made or become.

The present system of **fīō** is regular of the fourth conjugation, but the subjunctive imperfect is **fierem,** and the infinitive **fierī.**

	INDICATIVE	SUBJUNCTIVE
Present	**fīō, fīs, fit**	**fīam, fīas, fīat**
	(fīmus), (fītis), fīunt	**fīāmus, fīātis, fīant**
Imperfect	**fiēbam, fiēbās, etc.**	**fierem, fierēs, etc.**
Future	**fīam, fīes, etc.**	
Perfect	**factus sum**	**factus sim**
Pluperfect	**factus eram**	**factus essem**
Fut. Perf.	**factus erō**	

IMPERATIVE

(fī, fīte)

INFINITIVE

Present **fierī**   Perfect **factus esse**   Future **factum īrī**

PARTICIPLES

Perfect **factus, -a, -um**   Gerundive **faciendus, -a, -um**

Most compounds of **facio** with prepositions weaken ă to ĭ in the present stem and to ĕ in the supine stem, and are inflected regularly like verbs in -i:—**conficio, conficere, confeci, confectus,** finish, **conficior, confici, confectus.**

Other compounds retain **a,** and have **-fīō** in the passive: as **benefaciō, -facere, -fēcī, -factum;** passive **benefīō, -fierī, -factus,** benefit.

DEFECTIVE VERBS

Some verbs have lost the Present System, and use only tenses of the Perfect, in which they are inflected regularly. These are—

coepī, I began   **ōdī,** I hate   **meminī,** I remember

INDICATIVE

Perfect	**coepī**	**ōdī**	**meminī**
Pluperfect	**coeperam**	**ōderam**	**memineram**
Fut. Perf.	**coeperō**	**ōderō**	**meminerō**

SUBJUNCTIVE

Perfect	**coeperim**	**ōderim**	**meminerim**
Pluperfect	**coepissem**	**ōdissem**	**meminissem**

IMPERATIVE

			mementō
			mementōte

INFINITIVE

Perfect	**coepisse**	**ōdisse**	**meminisse**
Future	**coeptūrus esse**	**ōsūrus esse**	

192

| Perfect | coeptus, -a, -um | ōsus, -a, -um |
| Future | coeptūrus, -a, -um | ōsūrus, -a, -um |

The Perfect, Pluperfect and Future Perfect of **odi** and **memini** have the meanings of a Present, Imperfect, and Future respectively: —**odi,** I hate, **oderam,** I hated (was hating), **odero,** I shall hate.

VOCABULARY

A

a, ab: from or by.

abnego, -are, -avi, -atum: to deny, refuse.

abscedo, -cedere, -cessi, -cessum: to go away, depart.

absisto, -sistere, -stiti, -stitum: to go away; to desist from.

absolutio, -onis, f.: pardon; acquittal.

absolvo, -solvere, -solvi, -solutum: to free; to acquit.

absorbeo, -ere, -ui: to swallow up, to gulp down.

accedo, -ere, -cessi, -cessum: to come to, approach, draw nigh.

accendo, -ere, -cendi, -censum: to kindle.

acceptabilis: acceptable.

accipio, -ere, -cepi, -ceptum: to take, grasp, receive.

acclinis, -e: leaning on anything; inclined to.

acer, -cris, -cre: sharp, cutting.

actus, -us: motion; act.

ad: towards, to, at, in reference to.

addico, -ere, -dixi, -dictum: to assent to, promise, yield to.

adduco, -ere, -duxi, -ductum: to draw to oneself, to bring, lead, escort.

adhuc: yet, still, even now.

adeps, -dipis: the soft fat of animals.

adhaereo, -ere, -haesi, -haesum: to cling to, to hold fast to.

adjuto, -are, -avi, -atum: to help.

adjuvo, -are, -juvi, -jutum: to help, aid, assist.

adjutorium, -ii: help, aid, assistance.

admitto, -ere, -misi, -missum: to send to, to let go, to let in, to allow.

adoro, -are, -avi, -atum: to worship, adore.

adscribo, or ascribo, -ere, -scripsi, -scriptum: to write to, to attribute to, to enroll.

advenio, -ire, -veni, -ventum: to come, arrive.

adventus, -us: the coming; the first season of the ecclesiastical year.

adversus: opposed to, against, in the presence of.

advoco, -are, -avi, -atum: to summon, call, ask for help.

aduno, -are, -avi, -atum: to unite.

aequus, -a, -um: equal, level, fair, just.

aestimator, -oris: one who estimates, or appraises.

aestus, -us: heat.

aeternus, -a, -um: eternal, everlasting.

aeternalis, -e: eternal, everlasting.

affero, afferre, attuli, allatum: to bring to, to lead to.

affligo, -ere, -flixi, -flictum: to ill-treat, persecute.

agnus, -i: a lamb.

ago, -ere, -egi, -actum: to set in motion, do, act, deal with.

---

* In the Vocabulary, the fourth principal part of verbs is given ending in um, the supine form, as is usual in vocabularies. In the tables of conjugations and in the first part of the book, the Perfect Passive Participle was given instead, because the Supine itself is used so seldom, whereas the Perfect Passive Participle is used very frequently—the point of the last Principal Part is to give the Supine stem which can be obtained from either form.

aio (defective verb): to say.

aliquis, aliqua, aliquid: anyone; anything; something; someone.

altare, -is: an altar; high place for sacrifices.

altus, -a, -um: high; proud; lofty.

amarus, -a, -um: bitter.

ambigitur, from ambigo: it is gone about, one hestitates concerning.

ambulo, -are, -avi, -atum: to walk, to deport oneself.

amitto, -ere, -misi, -missum: to send away, to let go, to lose.

amor, -oris: love.

ancilla, -ae: handmaiden, attendant.

angelus, -i: angel, spirit, messenger.

anima, -ae: soul, life, spirit, heart.

animal, -alis: animal.

animosus, -a, -um: courageous, high-spirited, ardent.

anniversarium, -ii: anniversary.

annuntio, -are, -avi, -atum: to announce, proclaim, publish.

ante: before.

antiquus, -a -um: old, ancient.

antistis, or antistes -stitis: presiding priest. (One who stands before, lit.)

aperio, -ire, -perui, -pertum: to open, to reveal, expose.

appareo, -ere, -ui, -itum: to appear, come in sight.

appropinquo, -are, -avi, -atum: to approach, draw near.

apud: at, nearby, with, in the presence of, among.

aqua, -ae: water.

archangelus, -i: archangel.

ardeo, -ere, arsi, arsum: to glow, burn, be on fire.

argentum, -i: silver.

aridus, -a, -um: dry; arid.

ascendo, -ere, -scendi, -scensum: to ascend, go on high.

ascensio, -onis: an ascension.

asper, -a, -um: rough; harsh; bitter.

aspis, -idis: an asp, adder.

auctor, -oris: an originator, causer, doer.

audeo, -ere, ausus sum: to dare, venture.

audio, -ire, -ivi, -itum: to hear, listen to.

auditio, -onis: a hearing; a hearkening to.

aufero, auferre, abstuli, ablatum: to take or bear away, to destroy.

autem: but, on the contrary, however, moreover.

auxilium, -ii: aid, help.

ave: hail!

averto, -ere, -verti, -versum: to turn away, avert.

B

baculus, -i: a stick, staff, shepherd's staff.

basiliscus, -i: a basilisk, a kind of venomous serpent.

bibo, -ere, bibi, bibitum: to drink.

beatitudo, -inis: beatitude, happiness, bliss, blessedness.

beatus, -a, -um: blessed.

bene: well, rightly, uprightly.

benedico, -ere, -ixi, -ictum: to bless; to praise, thank.

benignus, -a, -um: kindly, favoring, loving.
bonus, -a, -um: good.
butyrum, -i: butter.

C

cado, -ere, cecidi, casum: to fall, bow down, fall prostrate.
caelestis, -e: heavenly, celestial.
caelum, -i or caeli, -orum: heaven; the heavens.
calculus, -i: a little stone, pebble.
calix, -icis: cup, goblet, chalice.
cano, -ere, cecini, cantum: sing, to celebrate in song.
canticum, -i: a song, a canticle.
capio, -ere, cepi, captum: to take possession of, obtain.
captivitas, -tatis: captivity.
caput, -itis: head.
caritas, -tatis: charity; love of one's neighbor for love of God.
caro, carnis: flesh; the body.
carus, -a, -um: dear, precious.
cassus, -a, -um: vain, empty, useless.
causa, -ae: cause; case (lawsuit).
cedo, -ere, cessi, cessum: to go, proceed; to yield.
cena, -ae: dinner, supper.
ceno, -are, -avi, -atum: to dine, to sup.
cernuus, -a, -um: falling headlong to the ground.
certus, -a, -um: certain, sure.
cibo, -are, -avi, -atum: to feed.
cibus, -i: food, nourishment.
cinis, -eris: ashes, ruins.
circumdo, -are, -dedi, -datum: to surround.
circumfulgeo, -ere, -fulsi: to shine roundabout: to encompass with
  radiance.
circumsto, -are, -steti: to stand round, to encircle.
cithara, -ae: a four-stringed instrument, the cithara.
civis, -is: a citizen.
civitas, -tatis: a city; citizenship.
clamo, -are, -avi, -atum: to cry aloud, to shout.
clamor, -oris: a loud shouting, a cry.
claresco, -ere, clarui: to grow bright, clear.
claritas, -tatis: clearness, brightness, brilliancy, renown.
claudo, -ere: to close, shut.
clemens, -entis: loving, merciful, clement.
clementia, -ae: kindness, mercy, clemency.
coaduno, -are, -avi, -atum: to unite closely, to knit together.
coeles, -itus: heavenly.
cogitatio, -onis: thinking, reflection, meditation, planning.
cogito, -are, -avi, -atum: to think, plan, consider.
cognatus, -a, -um: related, connected by blood.
cognosco, -ere, -gnovi, -gnitum: to become acquainted with, to know,
  to see.
cogo, cogere, coegi, coactum: to collect, to bring together.
cohaeres, -edis: co-heir.

collatio, -onis: a collection, contribution, present.

collaudo, -are, -avi, -atum: to praise very much.

colloco, -are, -avi, -atum: to place, set, put.

comedo, -ere, -edi, -esum: to consume entirely, to eat up.

commemoratio, -onis: commemoration, remembrance, mention.

commemoro, -are, -avi, -atum: to recollect, to remind, to mention.

commensalis, -is: a dinner companion, someone at the same table.

commercium, -ii: trade, commerce, communication.

commixtio, -onis: mixing together, mixture.

commoror, -ari, -atus sum: to delay, abide, dwell.

communio, -onis: communion.

compar, -aris: like, similar; an equal or companion.

comparo, -are, -avi, -atum: to make ready; to compare.

competenter: strivingly, fittingly.

complaceo, -ere, -cui or -citus sum: to please, find favor with.

comprehendo, -ere, -prehendi, -prehensum: to seize, to grasp; to comprehend.

comprimo, -ere, -pressi, -pressum: to squeeze, compress, to check.

concelebro, -are, -avi, -atum: to celebrate a festivity.

concipio, -ere, -cepi, -ceptum: to conceive, either physically or mentally.

conculco, -are, -avi, -atum: to tread under foot, to misuse.

condemnatio, -onis: condemnation; a sentence.

condicio, -onis: condition.

condo, -ere, -didi, -ditum: to lay up, store; to make, build.

condolesco, -ere, -dolui: to suffer severely.

confessio, -onis: confession; acknowledgment.

confido, -ere, confisus sum: to trust, believe firmly, be assured.

confiteor, -eri, confessus sum: to confess.

confirmo, -are, -avi, -atum: to strengthen, confirm, establish.

confuto, -are, -avi, -atum: to check, silence, confute.

cooperio, -ire, -perui, -pertum: to cover, envelop.

consecratio, -onis: consecration.

consecro, -are, -avi, -atum: to consecrate.

considero, -are, -avi, -atum: to look at, regard, consider.

consolator, -oris: consoler.

consolor, -ari, -atus sum: to comfort, encourage, console.

consors, -sortis: one having an equal share, partaker, sharer, consort.

consortio, -onis: companionship, community, partnership.

consortium, -ii: community of goods; fellowship, participation in.

conspectus, -us: look, view, survey.

conspicio, -ere, -spexi, -spectum: to view, descry, perceive.

consubstantialis, -e: consubstantial; being of one substance with.

contemplo, -are, -avi, -atum: to contemplate.

contero, -ere, -trivi, -tritum: to consume by rubbing away.

contineo, -ere, -tinui, -tentum: to keep together, bind, to contain, hold in check.

contingo, or **continguo:** to wet or moisten; **contingo:** to touch.

contristo, -are, -avi, -atum: to sadden, to make sad.

contritus, -a, -um: well-used, common, trite.

conturbo, -are, -avi, -atum: to disturb, throw into confusion.

conversatio, -onis: frequent use, frequent sojourn in a place, conversation.

conversatus, from converso: to turn round frequently.

converto, -ere, -verti, -versum: to turn, change, alter, refresh.

cor, cordis: the heart; mind, soul.

corpus, -oris: the body.

cotidianus, cotidie, quotidianus: daily.

creatura, -ae: anything created, rather than merely made. Wax, or salt, is a creature in this sense.

cremo, -are, -avi, -atum: to burn, consume by fire.

credo, -ere, -didi, -ditum: to believe, to trust.

creo, -are, -avi, -atum: to create, bring into being.

crucifigo, -ere, -ixi, -ixum: to crucify.

cruor, -oris: the blood which flows from a wound; slaughter.

crux, crucis: the cross.

culpa, -ae: fault, blame, error.

cultor, -oris: a cultivator, planter, laborer.

cum: with, together with; when, since, as soon as, although.

cunctus, -a, -um: all, the whole.

cura, -ae: care, solicitude, attention to, minding.

curo, -are, -avi, -atum: to take care of, to mind.

custodio, -ire, -ivi or ii, -itum: to guard, watch, keep.

custodia, -ae: a watch, guarding, custody.

D

daemonium, -ii: devil, demon, evil spirit.

damnatio, -onis: damnation, condemnation, a fine.

dator, -oris: giver.

de: from, away from, out of, in the course of, on account of.

debitor, -oris: a debtor.

debitus, -a, -um: bound, owed, due.

decem: ten.

decet, -ere, -uit: it becomes, it behooves, it is fitting.

decor, -oris: grace, elegance, beauty.

decorus, -a, -um: fitting, seemly, decorous.

deduco, -ere, -duxi, -ductum: to lead or bring down, to conduct, to despise.

defectus, -us: a failing, ceasing, disappearing.

defendo, -ere, -fendi, -fensum: to repel, guard, defend.

deficio, -ere, -feci, -fectum: to fail, waste away, pine for.

defunctus, see defungor.

defungor, defungi, defunctus sum: to finish, complete, discharge, be relieved of an office.

delectus, -us: a choice, selection, a levy.

deleo, -ere, -levi, -letum: to destroy, annihilate, abolish.

delictum, -i: fault, crime, delinquency.

delictus, from delinquo: to have been wanting in, having failed.

demum: at length, at last, now at last, then at last.

depositio, -onis: a putting, or taking, down.

deprecatio, -onis: prayer, supplication, entreaty.

deprecor, -ari, -atus sum: to pray earnestly, to entreat.

describo, -ere, -scripsi, -scriptum: to transcribe, to describe, to mark out.

desiderium, -ii: desire, yearning for, pining for.

desolatus, -a, -um: desolate.

desponsatus, from despondeo, -ere, -spondi, -sponsum: to promise, betroth.

desum; deesse, defui: to be absent, to be away, to be wanting.

desuper: from above, above.

deus, dei: God, a god. **dii, di, dei:** the gods.

devius, -a, -um: out of the way, erroneous.

devotio, -onis: a consecrating, devotion.

dexter, -era, -erum: on the right (hand).

dico, -are, -avi, -atum: to consecrate, dedicate, devote to.

dico, -ere, dixi, dictum: to say, tell, relate.

dies, -ei: a day.

digitus, -i: finger, digit.

digne: worthily.

dignitas, -tatis: worth, merit, dignity.

dignus, -a, -um: worthy, meritorious, befitting.

dignor, dignari, -atus sum: to deign.

dijudico, -are, -avi, -atum: to decide, discriminate, judge.

diligo, -ere, -lexi, -lectum: to love, prize, esteem highly.

dimitto, -ere, -misi, -missum: to send away, set free, discharge.

directus, -a, -um: straight, direct.

discerno, -ere, -crevi, -cretum: to separate, distinguish, discern.

discipulus, -i: disciple.

discutio, -ere, -cussi, -cussum: to disperse, scatter.

dissolutus, -a -um, from dissolvo, to scatter: having been scattered, dispersed.

dispar, -aris: unlike, different, disparate, not comparable.

dito, -are, -avi, -atum: to enrich, make wealthy.

diurnus, -a, -um: lasting for a day.

diversorium, (or deversorium) -ii: an inn, a lodging.

diversus, -a, -um: different, diverse, opposed.

divido, -ere, -visi, -visum: to divide, separate.

divinitas, -tatis: divinity, the divine.

divinus, -a, -um: divine, having to do with God.

do, -are, dedi, datum: to give, offer.

doceo, -ere, docui, doctum: to teach, instruct.

documentum, -i: example, warning, proof, document.

dogma, -atis: a statement of an accepted principle, usually theological.

doleo, -ere, dolui: to suffer, to grieve.

dolor, -oris: suffering, pain, grief, sorrow.

dolorosus, -a, -um: painful, grievous, sorrowful.

dolosus, -a, -um: deceitful, crafty.

domina, -ae: mistress of a household; lady.

dominus, -i: lord; master.

domus, -us: a house, household, home.

donec: as long as, while, until.

dono, -are, -avi, -atum: to give a present, to donate.

donum, -i: a gift, a present.

dormio, -ire, -ii, -itum: to sleep, slumber.

dormito, -are, -avi, -atum: to begin to sleep, to be lazy.

drachma, -ae: a small Greek coin.

draco, -onis: a snake, a dragon.

ductor, -oris: a leader or commander.

dulcedo, -inis: sweetness, charm. (Lit., a sweet taste.)

dum: while, as long as, until, provided that.

duodeni, -ae: twelve each, twelve.

dux, ducis: leader, guide, ruler, emperor.

E

ecce: behold, lo, see!

ecclesia, -ae: a church, The Church, an assembly, congregation.

edictum, -i: decree, edict.

edo, -ere, edi, esum: to eat.

edo, -ere, edidi, editum: to give out, to bring into the world, bring forth, give birth to.

educo, -ere, -duxi, -ductum: to lead out, to raise up, to educate.

efficio, -ere, -feci, -fectum: to produce, effect, make.

effundo, -ere, -fudi, -fusum: to pour out, pour forth, shed.

effulgeo, -ere, -fulsi: to shine forth, glitter.

ego: I.

ei: ah, woe!

eia: well then! quick! come then!

ejicio, -ere, -jeci, -jectum: throw out, drive out, cast out, eject.

electus, -a, -um: chosen, select, elect.

elevo, -are, -avi, -atum: to raise, lift up.

eligo, -ere, -legi, -lectum: choose, select.

emitto, -ere, -misi, -missum: to send forth, to stretch forth.

enarro, -are, -avi, -atum: to tell, narrate.

enim: for, certainly, indeed (never the first word in a clause).

eo, ire, ii, or ivi, itum: to go, proceed.

ergo: therefore, consequently.

eripio, -ere, -ripui, -reptum: to snatch away, tear out, pluck out.

erudio, -ire, -ivi or -ii, -itum: to teach, instruct.

eruo, -ere, -rui, -rutum: to dig out, to destroy, to raze.

esca, -ae: food, victuals.

et: and. et . . . et: both . . . and.

etiam: as yet, still, even, and again.

evangelium, -ii: the good tidings.

evangelizo, -are, -avi, -atum: to proclaim the good tidings.

eundem: the same. From **idem, eadem, idem.**

ex: also **e:** from, out of, from the time of.

exaudio, -ire, -ivi or -ii, -itum: to hear plainly, to listen to.

excelsus, -a, -um: lofty, high, elevated.

exeo, -ire, -ii, or -ivi, -itum: to go out, to go forth.

exercitus, -us: an army.

exhortor, -ari, -atus sum: to exhort, encourage.

eximius, -a, -um: exceptional, distinguished, extraordinary.

exitus, -us: a going forth, departure.

exoro, -are, -avi, -atum: to entreat, obtain by entreaty, to propitiate.

experior, -iri, expertus sum: to try, test; to learn by experience.

exprimo, -ere, -pressi, -pressum: to express to press out.

exsilium, -ii: exile, banishment.

exspecto, -are, -avi, -atum: to wait for, trust, await.

exsul, -sulis: an exile, a banished person.

exsultatio, -onis: a leaping up, exultation, great joy.

exsulto, -are, -avi, -atum: to leap up, to rejoice.

F

facies, -ei: the external form or figure, face, appearance.

facio, -ere, -feci, -factum: to make, prepare, build, fashion.

factor, -oris: a maker, creator.

famulus, -a, -um: serving. famulus, -i: a servant.

favilla, -ae: glowing ashes.

festivitas, -tatis: festivity.

fidelis, -e: trustworthy, faithful.

fides, -ei: trust, confidence, faith.

filius, -ii: a son, the son.

fingo, -ere, finxi, fictum: to fashion, form, mould.

finis, -is: boundary, territory; the end.

fio, fieri, factus sum: to be made, to become, to happen.

firmo, -are, -avi, -atum: to strengthen, to make firm.

flagellum, -i: a whip, a scourge.

flamma, -ae: a flame, blaze, blazing fire. flammeus, -a, -um: fiery, flaming.

flecto, -ere, flexi, flectum: to bend, to turn, to bow.

fleo, flere, flevi, fletum: to weep.

fletus, -us: weeping, bewailing.

foecundus, -a, -um, or fecundus: fruitful, productive.

fons, fontis: a fountain, spring.

foras: out, abroad, without, out of doors, outside.

forma, -ae: form, figure, shape, beauty.

formo, -are, -avi, -atum: to form, give shape to, fashion.

forte: perhaps, perchance.

fortis, -e: strong, mighty.

fortitudo, -inis: strength, might, fortitude.

foveo, -ere, fovi, fotum: to keep warm, to cherish, to favor.

fragilitas, -tatis: breakableness, fragility.

frango, -ere, -fregi, fractum: to shatter, to tame, to humble.

frater, fratris: a brother, cousin.

fremo, -ere, -ui, -itum: to growl, roar, murmur.

frequento, -are, -avi, -atum: to collect in large numbers, to visit frequently.

frigidus, -a, -um: cold, causing cold; inactive, remiss.

fructus, -us: enjoyment, produce, fruit, income.

fruitio, -onis: enjoyment, use, possession.

frumentum, -i: corn, i.e., wheat, rye, barley, etc.
futurus, -a, -um: future; about to be.

G

gaudeo, -ere, gavisus sum: to rejoice, to delight in.
gaudium, -ii: joy, gladness, delight.
generosus, -a, -um: of noble birth, noble, excellent.
genetrix, -tricis: a mother, the mother.
genitus (from gigno): having been born, brought forth.
gens, gentis: a clan, tribe, people, nation.
genus, generis: race, people, kind, class.
germino, -are, -avi, -atum: to sprout forth.
gero, -ere, gessi, gestum: to do, act, conduct oneself.
gigno, -ere, genui, genitum: to beget, bear, bring forth.
gladius, -ii: a sword, a short sword.
gloria, -ae: glory, renown, honor, majesty.
glorifico, -are, -avi, -atum: to give glory to, to praise.
gloriosus, -a, -um: glorious, full of glory.
gratia, -ae: grace, graciousness, courtesy, favor.
gratus, -a, -um: pleasing, agreeable.
grex, gregis: a herd, a flock, a troop.
guttur, -is: the throat.

H

habeo, -ere, -ui, -itum: to have, to possess, to hold.
habitaculum, -i: a dwelling-place, habitation.
habitatio, -onis: a habitation.
habito, -are, -avi, -atum: to inhabit, dwell in, abide.
haedus, -i: a kid, young goat.
haurio, -ire, hausi, haustum: to draw water, to drain (ex-haust).
hic, haec, hoc: this.
hinc: from here, hence; on this side, in this direction.
hodie: today, at the present time.
hodiernus, -a, -um: of, or relating to, today.
homo, -inis: man, the man.
honor, -oris: honor, distinction.
hospes, -itis: a guest, a guest friend.
hostia, -ae: a victim, sacrifice, offering, gift. (The Host.)
hostis, -is: an enemy; the enemy; the devil.
humanitas -tatis: human nature; humanity, kindness.
humanus, -a, -um: human, humane.
humilitas, -tatis: lowness, wretchedness, insignificance.
hymnus, -i: a song of praise to God.

I

ibi: there, at that place.
ideo: on that account, therefore.
igitur: so, therefore, then, accordingly.
ignis, -is: fire, a conflagration.
ignitus, -a, -um: tried by fire, purified from dross.
ille, illa, illud: that. Also: he, she, it.

illibatus, -a, -um: undiminished, uncurtailed, unimpaired.
illumino, -are, -avi, -atum: to make light, illumine.
illustratio, -onis: an illumining, illustration, making shine.
immaculatus, -a, -um: stainless, pure.
immortalitas, -tatis: deathlessness, immortality.
impietas, -tatis: sin, misdeed, transgression, impiety.
impingo, -ere, -pegi, -pactum: to strike, to beat against.
impius, -ii: (in plural): sinners, the godless, wicked.
impleo, -ere, -evi, -etum: to fill up, satiate, content.
impossibilis, -e: impossible.
in: in, into, to, in reference to, during.
incarnatio, -onis: incarnation, embodiment.
incensus, -a, -um: fiery, burning. incensum -i: incense.
inclytus, -a, -um: glorious.
incolatus, -us: a sojourn, a stay.
incolumitas, -tatis: safety, soundness, good condition.
incursus, -us: assault, attack.
indignus, -a, -um: unworthy, undeserving.
induco, -ere, -duxi, -ductum: to lead into, to bring into.
indulgentia, -ae: pardon, remission (of temporal punishment).
indulgeo, -ere, -dulsi, -dultum: to be indulgent, forbearing.
inebrio, -are, -avi, -atum: to fill up, inebriate, intoxicate.
infans, infantis: a babe, a child. (Lit. speechless.)
infernus, -i: the nether world, the kingdom of the dead, hell.
inferus, -i: same meaning as infernus.
infero, inferre, intuli, illatum: to bring in, to put or place on.
infimus, -a, -um: the lowest, the meanest, the lower world.
infundo, -ere, -fudi, -fusum: to pour into, infuse, impart.
ingemisco, -ere, ingemui: to sigh or groan.
ingredior, -gredi, -gressus sum: to enter, to go or come in.
inhabito, -are, -avi, -atum: to dwell, abide.
inhaereo, -ere, -haesi, -haesum: to cling to, to remain fast to.
inimicus, -a, -um: unfriendly, inimical. inimicus -i: an enemy.
iniquitas, -tatis: injustice, sin, iniquity.
iniquus, -a, -um: unjust, sinful.
innocens, -entis: harmless, guiltless, clean.
innoxius, -a, -um: harmless, innocent.
innumerabilis, -e: countless, numberless, innumerable.
insono, -are, -sonui, -sonitum: to sound, resound.
institutio, -onis: arrangement, instruction, the instituting of.
insto, -are, -stiti: to follow closely, to be close to.
intactus, -a, -um: untouched, intact, sound, pure, chaste.
inter: between, amongst, amid, during.
intercedo, -ere, -cessi, -cessum: to stand between, intercede.
intercessio, -onis: pleading on behalf of, intercession.
intimus, -a, -um: inmost.
intra: within, into, within the space or time of.
intro: within.
introeo, -ire, -ivi or -ii, -itum: to go into, enter.
introitus, -us: an entrance, beginning, introduction.

inultus, -a, -um: unavenged, unpunished.
invenio, -ire, -veni, -ventum: to find, to discover, come upon.
inviolatus, -a, -um: inviolate, uninjured, unhurt.
invisibilius, -a, -um: invisible.
invoco, -are, -avi, -atum: to call upon for help, to invoke.
involvo, -ere, -volvi, -volutum: to roll in, to wrap in, to roll along, to enfold.
ipse, -a, -um: himself, herself, itself. He, she, it.
is, ea, id: he, she, it. This or that person or thing.
iste, -a, -ud: this or that person or thing.
ita: so, thus, in such wise.
itaque: and so, and thus, therefore, for that reason.
item: also, likewise, in like manner.
iterum: again, a second time.

J

jam: now, already, just now, soon.
jubeo, -ere, jussi, jussum: to order, command.
jubiliatio, -onis: gladness, jubilation.
jubilo, -are, -avi, -atum: to rejoice, shout, sing.
jucundus, -a, -um: pleasing, acceptable, happy, fortunate.
judex, judicis: a judge.
judicium, -ii: a trial, investigation; a judgment; a law.
judico, -are, -avi, -atum: to judge, to do justice to.
jugiter: together, perpetually, continually, forever.
justitia, -ae: justice, righteousness, rectitude.
justus, -a, -um: just.
juventus, -tutis: youth.
juxta: near, close to, at hand, according to.

L

labia, -ae or labium -ii: a lip.
labor, -oris: work, labor, toil.
lacrimosus, -a, -um: tearful, mournful, pitiable.
lacus, -us: a pitfall, a trap, the grave, a lake.
laetifico, -are, -avi, -atum: to cheer, gladden, delight.
laetitia, -ae: joy, great and expressed delight.
laetor, -ari, -atus sum: to rejoice, be joyful.
lapis, -idis: a stone.
laqueus, -i: a noose, a snare, a net.
largior, -iri, -itus sum: to give abundantly, to bestow.
largitor, -oris: a liberal giver.
lassus, -a, -um: tired, faint, weary.
lateo, -ere, -ui: to be hidden, concealed.
latro, -onis: a robber, highwayman, brigand, thief.
latus, -a, -um: broad, wide. **latus -eris:** the side, the flank.
laudatio, -onis: praise, the praising of.
laudo, -are, -avi, -atum: to praise, to glorify.
laus, laudis: praise.
lavo, -are, lavi, lautum or lotum: to wash, bathe.

207

legalis, -e: legal, according to the law.

leo, leonis: lion.

lex, legis: a law, the law (of God).

liber, -era, -erum: free. liber, libri: a book.

libero, -are, -avi, -atum: to set free, to liberate.

lingua, -ae: tongue, language.

litera, -ae, (or littera): a letter, the letter.

locus, -i: a place.

longitudo, -inis: length.

longius: longer.

longus, -a, -um: long.

loquor, loqui, locutus sum: to speak, utter, tell.

luceo, -ere, luxi, luctum: to shine, glitter, give light.

lucifer, -era, -erum: light-bearing. lucifer, -feri: the morning star.

lugeo, -ere, luxi, luctum: to be mournful, to wear mourning.

lumen, -minis: light, brightness, splendor.

lux, lucis: light.

M

macula, -ae: spot, stain, mark.

magnus, -a, -um: great, large, tall, mighty.

majestas, -tatis: majesty, grandeur.

major, comparative of magnus: greater.

maledictus, -a, -um: accursed, cursed.

malus, -a, -um: bad, evil, wicked.

mandatum, -i: a law, precept, command, mandate.

mando, -are, -avi, -atum: to enjoin, order, command.

manduco, -are, -avi, -atum: to eat.

maneo, -ere, mansi, mansum: to abide, remain, continue.

manna, -ae: manna.

manus, -us: the hand. (Symbol of power and worth.)

mare, maris: the sea.

maximus, -a, -um: the greatest.

medela, -ae: a remedy, healing, cure.

meditor, -ari, meditatus sum: to think over, meditate.

medius, -a, -um: the middle, midmost, midst.

mel, mellis: honey.

memento: remember! from memini, meminisse: to remember.

memor, memoris: be mindful of, calling to mind.

memoria, -ae: memory, remembrance.

mens, mentis: the mind, soul, spirit.

mensa, -ae: table, the banquet or dinner-table.

mensis, -is: a month.

mereo, -ere, -ui, -itum; and mereor, mereri, meritus sum: to win,
  gain, earn, merit, be worthy of.

meridianus, -a, -um: of noonday, of midday.

merus, -a, -um: pure, unmixed with water: (said of wine).

meus, -a, -um: mine, my.

militia, -ae: military service, warfare, the military.

mille: a thousand. millia: thousands.

minuo, -ere, minui, minutum: to make smaller, less; to diminish.

mirabilis, -e: wonderful, marvellous.

mirabiliter: marvellously, wonderfully.

miror, -ari, -atus sum: to wonder at, to admire.

mirus, -a, -um: wonderful, astonishing, extraordinary.

miser, -era, -erum: miserable, wretched, pitiable.

miseratio, -onis: pity, compassion.

misereo, -ere, -serui, -seritum and -sertum; or, misereor, -eri, miseritus or misertus sum: to pity, to be sorry for.

misericordia, -ae: mercy, kindness, favor.

misericors, -cordis: merciful, abounding in mercy.

mitto, -ere, misi, missum: to send, let go, despatch.

modus, -i: measure, standard, mode, manner, fashion.

moereo, or maereo, -ere, -ui, -itum: to be sad, mournful.

molestus, -a, -um: burdensome, troublesome, annoying.

moneo, -ere, -ui, -itum: to remind, admonish, warn.

mons, montis: a mountain.

mora, -ae: a delay.

morior, mori, mortuus sum: to die.

mors, mortis: death.

mortalis, -e: mortal, subject to death.

mortuus, -a, -um: dead, having died.

moveo, -ere, movi, motum: to move, affect, influence.

mulier, mulieris: woman.

multitudo, -inis: a large number, multitude.

multus, -a, -um: many, much, numerous.

mundo, -are, -avi, -atum: to cleanse.

mundus, -a, -um: clean, pure.

mundus, -i: the world, universe, cosmos.

munio, -ire, -ivi or -ii, -itum: to build, fortify.

munus, muneris: a gift, present, a service.

mysterium, -ii: a secret, a secret knowledge, a holy mystery.

mysterius, -a, -um: having to do with the mystery.

mystice: mystically.

N

nam: for.

nativitas, -tatis: birth, nativity.

natura, -ae: nature, the nature.

natus, -a, -um: born; from **nascor, nasci, natus sum:** to be born.

ne: that not, lest.

negligens, -entis: negligent, careless.

negotium, -ii: business, occupation, employment.

nihil, also nil: nothing.

nimis: too much, overmuch, excessive.

nil: nothing.

nisi: if not, unless, except.

noceo, -ere, nocui, nocitum: to harm, hurt, injure.

nocturnus, -a, -um: by night, nightly.

nolo, nolle, nolui: to be unwilling, reluctant, to refuse.

nomen, nominis: a name.

non: not.

nosco, noscere, novi, notum: to become acquainted with, to know.
novus, -a, -um: new, fresh.
nox, noctis: night.
noxius, -a, -um: harmful, destructive.
nubes, -is: a cloud.
nullus, -a, -um: no one, no thing.
numen, numinis: the divine will, divinity.
numero, -are, -avi, -atum: to count, enumerate.
numquam: never.
numquid: a word indicating that a question is to follow.
nunc: now, at present.
nuntio, -are, -avi, -atum: to announce, tell, declare.

O

oblatio, -onis: offering, oblation.
obscurus, -a, -um: dark, obscure.
obsequium, -ii: compliance, obedience, submission.
observo, -are, -avi, -atum: to watch, observe, regard.
obumbratio, -onis: an overshadowing.
obumbro, -are, -avi, -atum: to overshadow, shield, protect.
oculus, -i: the eye.
odor, odoris: smell. Also **odos, odoris.**
offendo, -ere, -fendi, -fensum: to strike, knock; offend.
offensio, -onis: a striking against, a stumbling, a defeat, loss, misfortune.
offero, offerre, obtuli, oblatum: to present, offer, bring.
oleum, olei: olive oil, oil.
olim: formerly, once upon a time, at times.
omnipotens, -entis: all-powerful, almighty, omnipotent.
omnis, -e: all, every.
opportunus, -a, -um: opportune, fit, suitable.
optimus, -a, -um: best.
opus, operis: work, labor.
opus, est: there is need; it is necessary.
oratio, -onis: prayer, beseeching.
orbs, orbis: the globe, the world.
ordo, ordinis: order, the order (of the Masses).
orior, oriri, ortus sum: to rise, spring up, appear.
oro, orare, oravi, oratum: to pray, supplicate.
ortus, -us: a rising of heavenly bodies; the east.
os, oris: the mouth. **os, ossis:** bone.
ostendo, -ere, ostendi, ostentum: to show, display, expose.
ovis, -is: a sheep.

P

pacifico, -are, -avi, -atum: to make peaceful, to appease.
paenitet or poenitet, -ituit: it repents one, one relents.
palma, -ae: the palm tree, the palm of the hand; victory.
pango, -ere, panxi, panctum: to make, to undertake.
panis, -is: bread.
pannus, -i: a piece of cloth, swaddling clothes.

parcitas, -tatis: sparingness, moderation.
parco, parcere, peperci, parsum: to keep, preserve, spare.
pario, -ere, peperi, partum: to bear, bring forth.
pariter: likewise, similarly.
paro, -are, -avi, -atum: to prepare, make ready.
pars, partis: a part.
particeps, -cipis: a sharer, partaker.
participatio, -onis: a condition of being compact; a sharing.
partus, -us: a bearing, a bringing forth; birth.
par, paris: equal, like.
parum: too little, not enough.
pasco, -are, -avi, -atum: to feed, to pasture.
pascua, -ae: a pasture; grass land.
passio, -onis: suffering, the passion.
pastor, -oris: a shepherd.
pater, patris: a father.
paternus, -a, -um: fatherly, paternal.
patior, pati, passus sum: to suffer, bear with.
patro, -are, -avi, -atum: to accomplish, achieve.
pauper, -eris: poor, impoverished. The poor.
pax, pacis: peace.
peccator, -oris: a sinner.
peccatum, -i: a sin.
pecco, -are, -avi, -atum: to commit a sin, to sin.
pectus, -oris: the breast, the heart, seat of the affections.
pendo, -ere, pependi, pensum: to hang down, to depend on.
penna, -ae: a feather, a wing.
per: through, throughout, along, by means of.
perambulo, -are, -avi, -atum: to pass through, go about, traverse.
perceptio, -onis: a collecting; a perception; a partaking.
perdo, -ere, perdidi, perditum: to destroy, ruin.
perduco, -ere, -duxi, -ductum: to lead or bring through.
perennis, -e: lasting, perennial.
perfero, -ferre, -tuli, -latum: to carry through, to bear, suffer.
perfruor, -frui, -fructus sum: to enjoy thoroughly.
perhibeo, -ere, -ui, -itum: to bring forward, propose.
permaneo, -ere, -mansi, -mansum: to remain, abide.
permitto, -ere, -misi, -missum: to allow, to cede, to permit.
perpetuus, -a, -um: perpetual, everlasting.
pertranseo, -ire, -ivi or -ii, -itum: to pass through.
perturbatio, -onis: confusion, disorder, perturbation.
pervenio, -ire, -veni, -ventum: to arrive, to come to.
pervius, -a, -um: passable, having a road through, accessible.
pes, pedis: the foot.
peto, -ere, -ivi or -ii, -itum: to seek, ask for, beg for.
petra, -ae: a rock.
phantasma, -atis: an appearance, apparition.
pietas, -tatis: dutifulness, piety, compassion.
pius, -a, -um: acting dutifully, pious, virtuous.
placeo, -ere, -ui, -itum: to please, to be well pleasing.

plaga, -ae: a blow, stroke, wound.

planctus, -us: a lamentation.

plango, -ere, planxi, planctum: to bewail (striking the breast).

plebs, plebis: the people; the chosen people.

plenus, -a, -um: full, complete, entire.

pluo, -ere, plui: to rain.

poena, -ae: punishment, fine, expiation.

polluo, -ere, -ui, -utum: to defile, pollute.

pono, -ere, posui, positum: to place, put, lay, set.

populus, -i: the people, the populace.

porta, -ae: a gate, a city-gate.

porto, -are, -avi, -atum: to bear, carry.

posco, -ere, poposci: to ask earnestly, to beseech.

postquam: after, after that, as soon as.

potentia, -ae: power, ability, potency.

potestas, -tatis: power, might, strength.

potior, potiri, potitus sum: to get possession, obtain, become partaker of, have, be master of.

poto, -are, -avi, -atum or potum: to drink.

potus, -us: a drink, a draught.

praecedo, -ere, -cessi, -cessum: to go before, precede.

praeceptum, -i: a law, command, precept.

praeclarus, -a, -um: very bright, very brilliant, illustrious.

praedico, -are, -avi, -atum: to preach, make known publicly.

praefiguro, -are, -avi, -atum: to prefigure.

praegnans: full of, pregnant.

praeparo, -are, -avi, -atum: to make ready, prepare.

praesepium, -ii: a crib, a manger.

praesidium, -ii: a guard; protection, defence.

praesens, -entis: present, at hand.

praesentia, -ae: presence.

praesto, -are, -stiti, -stitum: to give, grant, furnish.

praesul, -sulis: a patron, a protector.

praesumo, -ere, -sumpsi, -sumptum: to take beforehand, to take for granted.

praeter: save, except, beyond, more than.

praeteritus, -a, -um: past, gone by.

praevius, -a, -um: going before, preceding.

precor, precari, precatus sum: to pray, beseech, entreat.

pretiosus, -a, -um: costly, precious.

pretium, -ii: a price, worth, value.

prex, precis: a prayer.

pridie: on the day before, yesterday.

primogenitus, -a, -um: first-born.

primus, -a, -um: first, foremost.

princeps, -cipis: the chief, the prince.

principium, -ii: the beginning, the principle.

prius: before, previously.

pro: before, in front of, on behalf of.

probo, -are, -avi, -atum: to test, examine, prove.

procedo, -ere, -cessi, -cessum: to go before, proceed.
procul: afar off, at a distance, far from.
profero, -ferre, -tuli, -latum: to bring forth, produce.
proficio, -ere, -feci, -fectum: to make progress, advance, to effect, avail, prevail.
profiteor, profiteri, professus sum: to acknowledge, profess.
profundus, -a, -um: profound.
promissio, -onis: a promise.
promitto, -ere, -misi, -missum: to promise, assure.
propitiabilis, -e: forgiving, forgivable.
propitio, -are, -avi, -atum: to soothe, appease.
propitius, -a, -um: favorably inclined, favorable.
propono, -ere, -posui, -positum: to set before, to prefer.
proprius, -a, -um: particular, personal, peculiar, own.
propter: near, hard by, on account of, because of.
prosum, prodesse, profui: to be useful, advantageous to.
protectio, -onis: protection.
protinus, or protenus: straightway, forward, further on.
provenio, -ire, -veni, -ventum: to come forth, prosper.
puer, pueri: a boy.
purgo, -are, -avi, -atum: to clean, purge.
purus, -a, -um: pure, undefiled.

Q

quaero, -ere, quaesivi, quaesitum: to seek, search for.
quaeso, -ere, -ivi or -ii: to beg, pray, beseech.
qualis, -e: of what sort; with talis, -e: of such sort . . . as.
quando: when.
quantus, -a, -um: how great, of what size; with tantus, -a, -um: of such size . . . that.
quasi: as it were, as if, a sort of.
-que: and. (It is always joined to some other word.)
qui, quae, quod: who, which, what, that.
quia: because.
quicumque, quaecumque, quodcumque: whoever, whichever, whatever.
quiesco, -ere, quievi, quietum: to rest, repose, be at peace.
quis, quid: who, what, anyone, anything.
quisquis, quaequae, quidquid: whoever, whichever, whatever.
quivis, quaevis, quidvis: whoever, whatever you will, anyone.
quod: because, on which acount, that.
quoniam: since, seeing that, whereas, because.
quoque: also.
quotiescumque: however often, as often as.
quotquot: however many.

R

radius, -ii: a staff, the spoke of a wheel, a ray or beam.
radix, -icis: a root.
ratio, -onis: a reason, account, reckoning.
ratus, -a, -um: reckoned, calculated, fixed, settled.

recedo, -ere, -cessi, -cessum: to retire, depart, recede.

recipio, -ere, -cepi, -ceptum: to receive, to take.

reclino, -are, -avi, -atum: to bend back, cause to lean back.

recolo, -ere, -colui, -cultum: to cultivate again, renew, repair.

recordor, -ari, -atus sum: to recall, remember, be mindful of.

recumbo, -ere, -cubui: to lie backwards, recline.

reddo, -ere, -didi, -ditum: to give forth, render what is due.

redemptio, -onis: redemption, being bought back.

redimo, -ere, -emi, -emptum: to redeem, ransom, rescue.

reduco, -ere, -duxi, -ductum: to lead back, bring back.

refectio, -onis: a restoring, repairing, refreshment.

reficio, -ere, -feci, -fectum: to refresh, restore.

reformo, -are, -avi, -atum: to remake, remould.

refraeno or refreno, -are, -avi, -atum: to restrain, hold back.

refrigerium, -ii: a cooling, refreshment; consolation.

refugium, -ii: a refuge, a place of refuge.

regina, -ae: a queen.

regio, -onis: a region, section, country, kingdom.

regno, -are, -avi, -atum: to reign over, rule.

rego, -ere, rexi, rectum: to rule, guide, direct.

religiosus, -a, -um: conscientious, god-fearing, pious.

relinquo, -ere, liqui, -lictum: to relinquish, leave.

reliquiae, -arum: the remains, relics, remnants.

remaneo, -ere, -mansi, -mansum: to remain, abide.

remedium, -ii: a remedy, cure.

remissio, -onis: forgiveness, pardon, remission.

repello, -ere, -puli, -pulsum: to drive back, away.

repleo, -ere, -evi, -etum: to fill up, replenish.

reposita from repono, -ere, -posui, -positum: put behind, make distant, to put in a repository.

repraesento, -are, -avi, -atum: to represent, to make manifest.

reprobo, -are, -avi, -atum: to disapprove, to reprobate.

requies, -ei: rest, resting-place.

requiesco, -ere, -quievi, -quietum: to rest, be at rest.

res, rei: thing, matter, object, circumstance.

respicio, -ere, -spexi, -spectum: to look, look upon, behold.

respondeo, -ere, -spondi, -sponsum: to answer, respond.

resurgo, -ere, -surrexi, -surrectum: to arise again.

resurrectio, -onis: resurrection, the resurrection.

resuscito, -are, -avi, -atum: to raise up again, restore.

retribuo, -ere, -tribui, -tributum: to repay, requite, reward.

retributio, -onis: repayment, retribution.

reus, -i: an accused, someone answerable for, guilty of.

rex, regis: a king.

rigidus, -a, -um: stiff, unbending, rigid.

rigo, -are, -avi, -atum: to moisten, wet, irrigate.

ritus, -us: a rite, religious custom, ceremony.

rogo, -are, avi, -atum: to pray, beseech, entreat.

roro, -are, -avi, -atum: to bedew.

rubeo, -ere, -ui, -itum: to grow red, to blush.

sacerdos, -dotis: a priest.

sacramentum, -i: a sacrament, the Eucharist.

sacrificium, -ii: an offering, oblation, sacrifice.

sacrosanctus, -a, -um: most holy, sacred.

saeclum or saeculum, -i: a lifetime, generation, age, eternity.

saecularis, -e: secular.

sagitta, -ae: an arrow.

salubris, -e: healthful.

salus, -utis: health, deliverance, temporal salvation.

salutaris, -e: healthful, beneficial, giving salvation. Also: a saviour, The Saviour.

salutatio, -onis: a salutation, greeting.

salutifer, -fera, -ferum: health-bringing, salutary.

salvator, -oris: a saviour, The Saviour.

salve: hail!

salvo, -are, -avi, -atum: to keep, save, preserve.

salvus, -a, -um: saved, safe.

sanctificator, -oris: the sanctifier.

sanctifico, -are, -avi, -atum: to sanctify, make holy.

sanctus, -a, -um: holy, sacred.

sanguis, -inis: blood.

sano, -are, -avi, -atum: to heal, make sound.

saturo, -are, -avi, -atum: to fill, satisfy, satiate.

saucius, -a, -um: wounded, injured, hurt.

scabellum, -i: a footstool.

scapulae, -arum: the shoulders.

scelus, -eris: wickedness, impiety, sin.

scio, -ire, -ivi, -itum: to know, understand.

scissura, -ae: a splitting, parting.

scribo, -ere, scripsi, scriptum: to write.

scutum, -i: a shield.

se: himself, herself, oneself.

sectator, -oris: a follower, a hanger-on.

secundus, -a, -um: following, second.

securus, -a, -um: secure, free from care.

sed: but, on the other hand, however.

sedeo, -ere, sedi, sessum: to rest, to sit.

sedes, -is: a seat, throne.

seipse: he, himself; (emphatic).

semen, -inis: seed.

semetipsum: himself; his very self (most emphatic).

semita, -ae: a path, way

semper: always, forever.

sempiternus, -a, -um: everlasting, eternal.

senectus, -tutis: age, old age.

sensus, -us: perception, sense, feeling.

sentio, -ire, sensi, sensum: to feel, perceive, sense.

septenarius, -a, -um: containing the number seven.

septiformis, -e: sevenfold, septiform.

sepulchrum, -i: a grave, tomb, sepulchre.
sepultus, -a, -um: buried.
sequentia, -ae: a sequence, a set of things following in order.
sequestro, -are, -avi, -atum: to deposit for safe-keeping.
serenus, -a, -um: calm, serene, clear, bright.
sermo, -onis: a word, speech, saying, discourse.
servitus, -tutis: slavery, servitude.
servo, -are, -avi, -atum: to save, preserve, guard.
servus, -i: a slave, a servant.
sextus, -a, -um: the sixth.
si: if, in case that, whether.
sic: so, thus, in this manner.
sicut: as, just as.
sicuti: another form of **sicut.**
sidus, -eris: a group of stars, a constellation, a single star.
signifer, -feri: the standard-bearer, leader, head.
signo, -are, -avi, -atum: to mark, sign, imprint.
signum, -i: a sign, a token.
similis, -e: like, similar to.
similiter: in like manner, similarly.
sincerus, -a, -um: pure, unmixed, sincere.
sine: without.
singulus, -a, -um: a single (person or thing).
sive: or if. **sive . . . sive:** whether . . . or; if . . . or . . .
sobrius, -a, -um: sober, not intoxicated.
societas, -tatis: society, company, association.
socio, -are, -avi, -atum: to combine, associate, share.
socius, -a, -um: taking part in, sharing.
sodalis, -is: a comrade, intimate, associate.
solatium, -ii: solace, consolation.
solus, -a, -um: alone, only.
somnium, -ii: a dream.
solvo, -ere, solvi, solutum: to loosen, untie, unbind, solve.
somnus, -i: sleep.
sonorus, -a, -um: sounding, sonorous.
sonus, -i: a noise, sound.
sordidus, -a, -um: dirty, filthy, unclean.
sors, sortis: fate, lot, destiny.
spargo, -ere, sparsi, sparsum: to scatter, besprinkle.
sparsus, -a, -um: spread out, scattered, sparse.
species, -ei: form, beauty, comeliness, appearance, kind.
speciosus, -a, -um: beautiful, splendid, dazzling.
spero, -are, -avi, -atum: to look for, expect, hope for.
spes, -ei: hope.
spiritus, -us: the breath, life, the spirit.
splendor, -oris: splendor, brilliance.
statuo, -ere, -ui, utum: to set up, cause to stand.
statura, -ae: height, size, stature.
status, -us: a standing, condition, state, status.
stella, -ae: a star.

sterilis, -e: sterile, barren.
sto, stare, steti, statum: to stand, remain standing.
strictus, -a, -um: drawn tight, severe, strict.
stupeo, -ere, stupui: to be stunned, stupefied.
suavis, -e: sweet, pleasant, agreeable, suave.
suavitas, -tatis: sweetness, pleasantness, suavity.
sub: under, during, near to.
subdo, -ere, -didi, -ditum: to subject, subdue.
subito: all at once, suddenly.
subsequor, -sequi, -secutus sum: to follow, follow after.
substantia, -ae: substance.
succensus, -a, -um: set on fire, ardent, burning.
sufficio, -ere, -feci, -fectum: to cause to grow up, to be adequate, to
   suffice.
sum, esse, fui: to be, to exist, to live.
sumo, -ere, sumpsi, sumptum: to take up, lay hold of, assume.
sumptio, -onis: a taking up, an assumption.
super: above, over, beyond, more than.
superbia, -ae: haughtiness, pride.
superfluus, -a, -um: superfluous.
supernus, -a, -um: above, over, on the top.
supervenio, -ire, -veni, -ventum: to come over, upon; to overtake.
supplementum, -i: a supplement, a fulfilling.
supplex, -icis: humbly begging; a suppliant.
supplicium, -ii: a kneeling down in entreaty; a punishment.
supplico, -are, -avi, -atum: to fall down on the knees before, entreat.
supra: above, over, on the top.
supremus, -a, -um: highest, greatest, most extreme.
surgo, -ere, surrexi, surrectum: to rise, to arise.
susceptor, -oris: a protector, helper, defender.
suscipio, -ere, -cepi, -ceptum: to guard, protect, defend.
suspiro, -are, -avi, -atum: to sigh, to long for.
suus, -a, -um: his, her, its own; their own.

T

tabernaculum, -i: a tent, a pavilion, a tabernacle.
tam: so far, to such a degree; tam . . . quam . . . to such a degree . . .
   as . . .
tamquam: as, as if, as it were, just as if.
tango, -ere, tetigi, tactum: touch, touch upon.
tantum: so much, only.
tartarus, -i: the infernal regions.
tectum, -i: a roof, an abode, dwelling.
temporalis, -e: temporal, lasting for a time.
temperies, -ei: a proper mixture, organization.
tempero, -are, -avi, -atum: to set proper bounds to, to rule, govern.
tempus, -oris: time.
tenebrae, -arum: the shadows; darkness, affliction.
tentatio, -onis: a trial, a temptation.
tento, -are, -avi, -atum: to try, to tempt.

217

terminus, -i: a boundary mark, limit, terminus, end.
tero, -ere, trivi, tritum: to wear out, rub to pieces, destroy.
terra, -ae: the earth.
terrestris, -e: terrestrial, of the earth.
testamentum, -i: testament, written witness.
testimonium, -ii: witness, testimony. Also: laws, commandments.
testis, -is: a witness.
thronus, -i: a throne.
timeo, -ere, -ui: to fear, to be afraid of.
timor, -oris: fear, reverence.
tollo, -ere, sustuli, sublatum: to take away, to bear away.
tormentum, -i: torture; a rack.
totus, -a, -um: the whole, all, entire.
trado, -ere, -didi, -ditum: to give up, hand over, deliver.
transeo, -ire, -ivi or -ii, -itum: to go across, to pass by, visit.
tremo, -ere, -ui: to tremble, quake.
tremor, -oris: trembling.
tribulatio, -onis: tribulation, affliction.
tribulo, -are, -avi, -atum: to oppress, afflict.
tribuo, -ere, -ui, -utum: to grant, give, bestow.
trinitas, -tatis: the Trinity.
tristis, -e: sad, sorrowful, dejected.
tu: thou, you.
tuba, -ae: a trumpet.
tunc: then, at that time.
turba, -ae: a crowd; tumult.
turbo, -are, -avi, -atum: to trouble, disturb, throw into disorder.
tutamentum, -i: defence, protection.
tuus, -a, -um: thy, thine, your (sing).

U

ubi: where.
ubique: wherever, everywhere.
ultio, -onis: an avenging, a punishment.
umbra, -ae: a shade, a shadow.
unctio, -onis: unction, an anointing.
unde: whence, wherefore.
unigenitus: the Only-Begotten.
unitas, -tatis: unity.
universus, -a, -um: whole, entire, all.
unus, -a, -um: one.
uro, -ere, ussi, ustum: to burn.
ut: that, in order that, as, like.
uter, -tra, -trum: each of two, both.
uterus, -i: the womb.
uti, see **ut.**
utilitas, -tatis: utility, usefulness.
uxor, oris: a wife.

V

vacillo, -are, -avi, -atum: to totter, reel, stagger, waver.
valde: very, very much, exceedingly.
vale: farewell!
valeo, -ere, -ui, -itum: to be strong, to avail, to prevail.
validus, -a, -um: strong, powerful.
vallis, -is: a vale, valley.
vallum, -i: a wall.
vanitas, -tatis: vanity, emptiness, unreality.
vanus, -a, -um: vain, empty, void.
vecors, vecordis: silly, foolish, mad, senseless.
vel: or, and also. **vel . . . vel:** either . . . or.
venerabilis, -e: venerable, to be revered.
veneror, -ari, -atus sum: to reverence, to venerate.
venia, -ae: grace, indulgence, favor.
venio, -ire, veni, ventum: to come, to happen.
venor, venari, venatus sum: to hunt, to pursue, strive after.
venter, -tris: the womb.
verbum, -i: a word; The Word.
vere: truly.
veritas, -tatis: truth.
verumtamen: but yet, notwithstanding, nevertheless.
verus, -a, -um: true.
vester, -tra, -trum: your, yours (Plural).
via, -ae: a way, path, road.
viator, -oris: a wayfarer, traveller.
victoria, -ae: victory.
video, -ere, vidi, visum: to see, to catch sight of.
vigilia, -ae: vigil, a watch by night.
vigilo, -are, -avi, -atum: to watch by night, to be on guard.
vinculum, -i: a yoke, a bond, fetters.
vinum, -i: wine.
vir, viri: a man.
virga, -ae: a rod, a wand; a slip for planting.
virginitas, -tatis: virginity.
virgo, virginis: a virgin, The Virgin.
virtus, -tutis: virtue, valor, strength, courage.
vis, vis, plural **vires:** force, power, strength, influence.
viscera, -erum: the bowels, the inmost parts of anything.
visibiliter: visibly.
visito, -are, -avi, -atum: to visit as a manifestation of Divine favor or wrath.
visus, -us: sight.
vita, -ae: life, vitality.
vito, -are, -avi, -atum: to avoid, shun.
vivfico, -are, -avi, -atum: to quicken, give life to, vivify.
vivo, -ere, vixi, victum: to live, to be alive.
vix: hardly, scarcely.
voco, -are, -avi, -atum: to call, summon.

219

volo, -are, -avi, -atum: to fly, as a bird.
volo, velle, volui: to will, wish, desire.
voluntas, -tatis: will, wish, desire.
vos, plural of **tu:** ye, you.
votum, -i: a vow.
vox, vocis: the voice, the sound of an instrument.
vulnero, -are, -avi, -atum: to wound.
vulnus, vulneris: a wound.
vultus, -us: the countenance, expression of the face, the face.

———

INDEX

221